Teaching Pyramid Observation Tool (TPOT™) for Preschool Classrooms Manual, Research Edition

Teaching Pyramid Observation Tool (TPOT™) for Preschool Classrooms Manual, Research Edition

Mary Louise Hemmeter, Ph.D.
Vanderbilt University
Nashville, Tennessee

Lise Fox, Ph.D.
University of South Florida
Tampa

and

Patricia Snyder, Ph.D.
University of Florida
Gainesville

Baltimore • London • Sydney

Paul H. Brookes Publishing Co.
Post Office Box 10624
Baltimore, Maryland 21285-0624
USA

www.brookespublishing.com

Typeset by Cenveo Publisher Services, Columbia, Maryland.
Manufactured in the United States of America by
Versa Press Inc., East Peoria, Illinois.

The individuals described in this book are composites or real people whose situations are masked and are
based on the authors' experiences. In all instances, names and identifying details have been changed to protect
confidentiality.

The TPOT™ was based in part on work conducted through the following grants. However, the opinions expressed
do not necessarily reflect the position or policy of the United States Department of Education or the United States
Department of Health and Human Services, and no official endorsement by either department should be inferred.

The Center on the Social Emotional Foundations for Early Learning, United States Department of Health and
Human Services, Grant Number 90YD0215/01.

The Technical Assistance Center on Social Emotional Intervention for Young Children, Office of Special Education Programs, United States Department of Education, Grant Number H326B070002.

*Examining the Potential Efficacy of a Classroom Wide Model for Promoting Social Emotional Development and
Addressing Challenging Behavior in Preschool Children With and Without Disabilities,* Institute of Education
Sciences, United States Department of Education, Grant Number R324A070212.

*Examining the Efficacy of a Classroom Wide Model for Promoting Social Emotional Development and Address-
ing Challenging Behavior in Preschool Children With or At-Risk for Disabilities,* Institute of Education Sciences,
United States Department of Education, Grant Number R324A120178.

Library of Congress Cataloging-in-Publication Data

Hemmeter, Mary Louise.
   Teaching pyramid observation tool (TPOT) for preschool classrooms manual : research edition / by Mary Louise
Hemmeter, Ph. D., Lise Fox, Ph.D., and Patricia Snyder, Ph.D.
      pages   cm
   Includes bibliographical references and index.
   ISBN 978-1-59857-283-4
   1. Education, Preschool—United States—Evaluation. I. Fox, Lise. II. Snyder, Patricia, 1955 July 13- III. Title.

   LB1140.23.H44 2013
   372.21—dc23
                                                                                        2013027377

British Library Cataloguing in Publication data are available from the British Library.

Contents

About the Authors

Mary Louise Hemmeter, Ph.D., is a professor in the Department of Special Education at Vanderbilt University. She teaches courses, advises students, and conducts research on early childhood issues. She is the cofaculty director of the Susan Gray School for Children, which is an early childhood program for children with and without disabilities. Her research focuses on effective instruction, social–emotional development and challenging behavior, translating research to practice, and effective approaches to professional development. Currently, she directs an Institute of Education Sciences–funded research project focused on the efficacy of implementing the Teaching Pyramid in classrooms, and she works on the National Center on Quality Teaching and Learning and the Office of Special Education Programs–funded Technical Assistance Center on Social Emotional Interventions. She is a coeditor of the *Journal of Early Intervention* and serves on the editorial boards of other major journals in early childhood special education. She served as President of the Council for Exceptional Children's Division for Early Childhood (DEC) and received the Merle B. Karnes award from DEC.

Lise Fox, Ph.D., is a professor in the Department of Child and Family Studies of the University of South Florida in Tampa, Florida, and the codirector of Florida Center for Inclusive Communities: A University Center for Excellence in Developmental Disabilities (www.flcic. org). She was the principal investigator of the Technical Assistance Center for Social Emotional Intervention (www.challengingbehavior.org) funded by the Office of Special Education Programs. Dr. Fox is engaged in research and training efforts related to the implementation of the *Pyramid Model* in early education and care classrooms, program-wide models of implementation, and positive behavior support. She received the Mary E. McEvoy Service to the Field Award from the Division for Early Childhood.

Patricia Snyder, Ph.D., is the David Lawrence Jr. Endowed Chair in Early Childhood Studies and Director of the Center for Excellence in Early Childhood Studies at the University of Florida. She has more than 35 years experience in early intervention and early childhood as a direct service provider, program administrator, faculty member, and researcher. She is former editor of the *Journal of Early Intervention* and is an associate editor for *Topics in Early Childhood Special Education*. Her research focuses on embedded instruction for early learning, young children's social-emotional competence, professional development, and measurement of early childhood outcomes. She has been a principal investigator or coprincipal investigator for a number of funded research and technical assistance projects focused on these research emphasis areas. Dr. Snyder has authored more than 85 articles and book chapters, has served on the editorial boards for seven professional journals, and presented more than 400 seminars, workshops, and presentations at state, national, and international conferences. She served two terms as a principal member of the early intervention and early learning in special education review panel for the Institute of Education Sciences; is a member of the Division for Early Childhood Recommended Practices Commission; and has received numerous awards for her research, teaching, and service contributions to the field, including the Mary E. McEvoy Service to the Field and Merle B. Karnes Service to the Division awards from the Division for Early Childhood of the Council for Exceptional Children.

Acknowledgments

The Teaching Pyramid Observation Tool (TPOT™) was developed as part of our work on two nationally funded centers: The Center on the Social and Emotional Foundations for Early Learning and the Technical Assistance Center on Social Emotional Interventions for Young Children. We would like to acknowledge the contributions of the individuals who worked with us on conceptualizing the *Pyramid Model*. Their knowledge, experiences in the field, and passion for supporting young children were instrumental in supporting our work on the TPOT. They include Judy Carta, Rob Corso, Glen Dunlap, Amy Hunter, Gail Joseph, Roxane Kaufmann, Rochelle Lentini, Micki Ostrosky, Amy Santos, Barbara Smith, Phil Strain, Matt Timm, and Tweety Yates.

In addition, many students and staff worked on our funded research projects that supported the development of and research on the TPOT. They asked questions, made suggestions, provided feedback, and supported our work in ways that greatly enhanced the TPOT. Special thanks are extended to Denise Perez Binder, Crystal Bishop, Cinda Clark, Shelley Clarke, Jill Grifenhagen, Alana Griffin, Beverly Hand, Jessica Hardy, Amanda Higgins, Kiersten Kinder, Tara McLaughlin, Kathleen Artman Meeker, Jessie Morris, Emily Robinson, Jenna Shepcaro, and Myrna Veguilla. We have greatly appreciated the support of James Aligna and M. David Miller during the initial validation of the TPOT.

Although it is not possible to list all the administrators, teachers, and other personnel who supported our TPOT research in their programs, we would like to acknowledge their willingness to support our work and express our thanks to them through our dedication.

*To the programs and teachers who work tirelessly to support
young children and their families, professional development personnel and
administrators who work every day to support teachers and others who work with
children and families, and to our staff and colleagues who support us every day in the work we do*

CHAPTER 1

Introduction to the
Teaching Pyramid Observation Tool

The *Teaching Pyramid Observation Tool (TPOT™) for Preschool Classrooms, Research Edition*, is an instrument designed to measure practitioners' implementation of teaching and behavior support practices associated with the *Pyramid Model for Promoting Social Emotional Competence in Infants and Young Children* (Fox, Dunlap, Hemmeter, Joseph, & Strain, 2003; Hemmeter, Ostrosky, & Fox, 2006). The *Pyramid Model* (see Figure 1.1) is a multitiered framework that organizes empirically supported teaching practices for promoting social-emotional competence and addressing challenging behavior of preschool children. The development of the *Pyramid Model* was influenced by public health models of promotion, prevention, and intervention practices (Gordon, 1983; Simeonsson, 1991) and schoolwide multitiered systems of positive behavior intervention and supports (Horner, Sugai, Todd, & Lewis-Palmer, 2005; Walker et al., 1996). The *Pyramid Model* includes universal, secondary, and tertiary teaching practices to support the social-emotional competence of all children, the provision of targeted supports for children at risk, and the inclusion of individualized interventions for children with persistent challenges (Fox et al., 2003; Fox, Carta, Strain, Dunlap, & Hemmeter, 2010; Hemmeter et al., 2006; Powell, Dunlap, & Fox, 2006). The first tier of the *Pyramid Model* emphasizes universal practices related to nurturing and responsive relationships and high-quality supportive classroom environments; the second tier focuses on explicit social, emotional, and behavioral teaching practices; and the third tier focuses on an assessment-based process that results in the development of individualized behavior support plans.

The *Pyramid Model* was developed by two national centers, the Center on the Social and Emotional Foundations for Early Learning (CSEFEL) and the Technical Assistance Center on Social Emotional Interventions (TACSEI). Through these two centers, teachers[1] in all 50 states have received training on the *Pyramid Model*. More than 5,000 trainers and 2,500 coaches have been trained to use a professional development approach to support the implementation of the *Pyramid Model* by early childhood practitioners. State reports on efforts toward systematic implementation, the integration of the model into programs, and the satisfaction of program staff with the model are available on both centers' web sites (http://www.challengingbehavior.org and http://www.vanderbilt.edu/csefel).

The *Pyramid Model* intervention was evaluated in a potential efficacy trial (Hemmeter, Snyder, Fox, & Algina, 2011). In this study, 40 teachers were randomly assigned to either an intervention condition or a business-as-usual control condition. Teachers in the intervention condition attended workshops to learn about the *Pyramid Model*

---

[1]Throughout this manual, we will use the term "teachers" to refer to individuals who work with children in preschool classrooms. This includes public school pre-kindergarten teachers, child care providers, Head Start teachers, early childhood educators, and others who work directly with children.

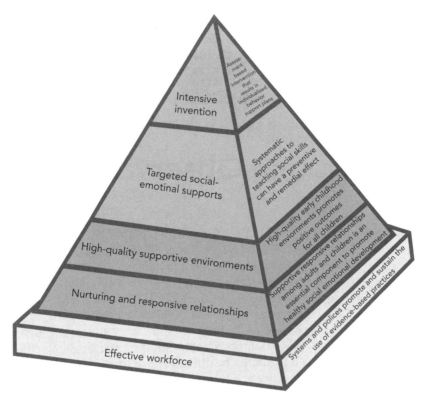

Figure 1.1. *Pyramid Model* framework. (From Center on Social and Emotional Foundations for Early Learning at Vanderbilt University. [2003]. *Pyramid model for promoting social and emotional competence in infants and young children.* Nashville, TN: Author.)

and associated teaching practices and received coaching in their classrooms to support implementation of the practices. In the classrooms of the teachers in the intervention condition, there were statistically significant and noteworthy improvements in children's social skills. Target children (children identified as having persistent challenging behavior) in *Pyramid Model* intervention classrooms had statistically significant and meaningful decreases in challenging behavior based on teacher ratings and were observed to have meaningful improvements in positive social interactions.

ORGANIZATION OF THE TPOT MANUAL

The TPOT manual provides background information on the *Pyramid Model for Promoting Social Emotional Competence in Infants and Young Children* (Fox et al., 2003; Hemmeter et al., 2006) and the use of the TPOT™ to measure the fidelity with which teachers implement *Pyramid Model* practices. This manual is designed to provide guidance to users on how to administer and score the TPOT and how to interpret the results. We describe each of the items, provide scoring guidance, and define terms that are relevant to using the TPOT. Case studies that demonstrate how the TPOT can be used to coach individual teachers as well as plan program-wide professional development activities are provided. The manual also provides answers to frequently asked questions about the TPOT. Finally, the manual includes information on the psychometric integrity of the TPOT and how the TPOT has been used in research.

ORGANIZATION OF THE TPOT

The TPOT was developed to provide an objective way to measure the fidelity with which preschool teachers implement *Pyramid Model* teaching practices, including universal practices associated with nurturing and responsive relationships and high-quality supportive classroom environments, targeted social-emotional and behavioral support teaching practices, and practices that demonstrate teachers' capacity to individualize social-emotional or behavioral interventions for children with persistent social, emotional, or behavioral challenges.

The TPOT has three parts organized as subscales. Subscale 1 has 14 key teaching practice items derived from the *Pyramid Model* frame work. Observable indicators are organized under each key practice. The key practices items are derived from the *Pyramid Model* framework. The 14 key practice items are 1) schedules, routines, and activities; 2) transitions between activities; 3) supportive conversations; 4) promoting children's engagement; 5) providing directions; 6) collaborative teaming; 7) teaching behavior expectations; 8) teaching social skills and emotional competencies; 9) teaching friendship skills; 10) teaching children to express emotions; 11) teaching problem solving; 12) interventions for children with persistent challenging behavior; 13) connecting with families; and 14) supporting family use of *Pyramid Model* practices. The number of practice indicators associated with each item varies from 5 to 10. There are a total of 114 practice indicators in this part of the TPOT. Subscale 2 of the TPOT includes 17 red flags. Red flags are indicators of poor structural and interactional quality in the classroom environment that conflict with or impede the implementation of *Pyramid Model* practices. When *Pyramid Model* practices are implemented with fidelity, no red flags would be observed. Subscale 3 of the TPOT is an item focused on using effective strategies to respond to challenging behavior. It includes three essential practices that teachers should use in response to incidences of challenging behavior in the preschool classroom. This part of the TPOT is used only when challenging behavior occurs during a TPOT observation.

POTENTIAL USES FOR THE TPOT

The TPOT can be used in several ways. First, it can be used in research to characterize descriptively the fidelity of implementation of *Pyramid Model* practices in a classroom, a group of classrooms in a program, or a group of programs in an organization, region, or state. The TPOT can also be used to address research questions focused on evaluating the extent to which the fidelity of practice implementation changes after an intervention or the extent to which the fidelity of practice implementation is associated with teacher or child variables of interest, such as a teacher's self-efficacy or a child's social, emotional, behavior, or preacademic skills. Second, the TPOT can be used in professional development or technical assistance activities to provide information about which practices are or are not being implemented in a classroom, a group of classrooms in a program, or a group of programs in an organization, region, or state. The need for training, coaching, or other implementation supports can be identified based on information obtained from the TPOT. The TPOT can be used repeatedly with teachers as coaching or other supports are provided to document progress in practice implementation, or change in fidelity of implementation can be evaluated in relation to the type and intensity of implementation supports provided. Third, the TPOT can be used in program improvement or quality rating initiatives as a measure of classroom or program quality related to the *Pyramid Model* practices.

ADMINISTRATION OF THE TPOT

The administration of the TPOT includes an observation and an interview. The duration of observation should be 2 hours. Teacher-directed activities (e.g., large-group circle, small-group instruction), child-directed activities (e.g., center time, free play), and the transitions that occur between activities are observed. In addition, a 15- to 20-minute structured interview with the teacher is conducted using the questions provided for certain key practice items and two red flags.

When administering the TPOT, the observer will use a scoring form. The form includes instructions for completing the observation, a place to note the start and ending time of the observation, a place to make notes about the children and adults present in the classroom during the observation, a chart for tracking the schedule of the classroom, and each part of the TPOT to be completed during the observation. Space for making notes during the observation and writing answers during the interview is also provided on the scoring form. The scoring form includes a scoring summary sheet for summarizing the scores across each part of the TPOT and constructing a summary score profile.

RESEARCH ON THE TPOT

The TPOT has been or is being used in a number of studies, either as a measure of the effects of a professional development intervention on teacher implementation of *Pyramid Model* practices or as a descriptive measure of teacher implementation of *Pyramid Model* practices. These studies are described in this section. Studies related to the technical adequacy of TPOT scores are described in Chapter 7.

In addition to the potential efficacy trial previously described (Hemmeter et al., 2011), a randomized controlled trial of the *Pyramid Model* intervention is being conducted with 84 preschool teachers (Hemmeter, Fox, Snyder, & Algina, 2012). In this study, teachers are randomly assigned to an intervention or business-as-usual control condition. Teachers in the intervention condition receive a professional development intervention designed to support their implementation of *Pyramid Model* practices. The professional development intervention includes high-quality workshops, implementation materials, and weekly coaching. The TPOT is being used both as a measure of teacher implementation of *Pyramid Model* practices across conditions and as a tool for coaching teachers in the intervention condition.

The utility of the TPOT for providing coaching to teachers implementing the *Pyramid Model* and associated teaching practices has been demonstrated in several studies. Fox and colleagues conducted a study with three early childhood special education teachers in classrooms that enrolled children with and without disabilities (Fox, Hemmeter, Snyder, Binder, & Clarke, 2011). In this study, the TPOT was used to assess changes in teacher implementation of the *Pyramid Model* practices as a result of weekly coaching. Teachers were coached to use practices associated with each tier of the *Pyramid Model* sequentially. In a follow-up study with three preschool teachers (Schnitz, Hemmeter, Hardy, Adams, & Kinder, 2011), the TPOT was used to identify areas in which teachers needed assistance. Based on TPOT implementation scores, three practices were selected on which teachers received coaching. TPOT items associated with these practices were used to monitor teachers' progress toward higher levels of implementation. Further, the TPOT was conducted before and after intervention to determine if there were changes in overall TPOT scores based on the coaching intervention. Artman-Meeker, Hemmeter, and Snyder (2013) used the TPOT in a study examining the use of distance coaching to support Head Start teachers' implementation of *Pyramid Model* practices. The TPOT was conducted at four points in time prior to, during, and at the end of the intervention to document teacher growth as a result of distance coaching.

Steed and Durand (2013) used the TPOT in a study on the differential impact of two professional development interventions on preschool teachers' use of positive behavioral interventions and supports (PBIS) and on young children's social-emotional issues.

Teachers were randomly assigned to either optimistic teaching or traditional PBIS coaching. The TPOT was used to measure teachers' use of PBIS strategies.

The TPOT has also been used to inform the development of protocols used for interviews, surveys, and document analysis. Snell and colleagues (Snell, Berlin, Voorhees, Stanton-Chapman, & Hadden, 2012; Snell et al., 2012) used the TPOT in a series of studies designed to understand the practices that Head Start staff used for addressing challenging behavior. The TPOT was used in two different ways in these studies. First, the items on the TPOT informed the development of a survey tool and interview protocol about teachers' use of practices related to challenging behavior. Second, the TPOT was used to observe teachers' classroom practices as a follow-up to the surveys and interviews.

Quesenberry, Hemmeter, and Ostrosky (2011) examined Head Start policies and procedures related to strategies for preventing and addressing challenging behavior. In this study, they developed a rubric for evaluating the policies and procedures. The TPOT was used to inform the development of the rubric and the interview protocol that was used to collect information about the policies and procedures.

The TPOT has been used as a descriptive measure in several studies. Morris (2012) used the TPOT as a descriptive measure of preschool classrooms in which teachers were being trained to implement individualized behavior supports for children with ongoing persistent, challenging behavior. In this study, the TPOT was used to describe the extent to which universal practices were in place as a context for implementing individualized behavior support plans. Artman-Meeker and Hemmeter (2013) used the TPOT as a descriptive measure in a study focused on coaching teachers to use prevention practices associated with the *Pyramid Model*. In this study, the TPOT was used to describe the status of *Pyramid Model* implementation in the teachers' classrooms prior to intervention.

Branson and Demchak (2011) used the TPOT in a study examining the use of *Pyramid Model* practices by teachers in toddler classrooms and the relationship between the use of these practices and overall classroom quality. They used the TPOT to measure teachers' use of *Pyramid Model* practices and the Early Childhood Environment Rating Scale (Harms, Clifford, & Cryer, 1998) to examine overall classroom quality.

These studies illustrate the use of the TPOT for several different purposes, including professional development, research, and program evaluation. In the next chapter, we describe the *Pyramid Model*, the practices associated with the model, and the processes and procedures used to develop and refine the TPOT.

CHAPTER 2

Overview of the *Pyramid Model* and the Teaching Pyramid Observation Tool

The development of the *Pyramid Model* was influenced by public health models of promotion, prevention, and intervention practices (Gordon, 1983; Simeonsson, 1991) and multi-tiered systems of positive behavior interventions and supports (Horner, Sugai, Todd, & Lewis-Palmer, 2005; Walker et al., 1996). Similar to public health frameworks, the *Pyramid Model* includes universal, secondary, and tertiary practices to ensure the social-emotional competence of all children, the provision of targeted supports to children at risk, and the inclusion of interventions for children with persistent social or behavioral challenges (Fox, Dunlap, Hemmeter, Joseph, & Strain, 2003; Hemmeter, Ostrosky, & Fox, 2006; Powell, Dunlap, & Fox, 2006). The teaching practices associated with the *Pyramid Model* are based on research on effective instruction for young children (Burchinal, Vandergrift, Pianta, & Mashburn, 2010; National Research Council, 2001), strategies to promote child engagement and appropriate behavior (Chien et al., 2010; Conroy, Brown, & Olive, 2008), the promotion of children's social skills (Brown, Odom, & McConnell, 2008; Vaughn et al., 2003), and the implementation of individualized assessment-based behavior support plans for children with the most severe social, emotional, and behavioral needs (Blair, Fox, & Lentini, 2010; Conroy, Dunlap, Clarke, & Alter, 2005; McLaren & Nelson, 2009).

Tier 1: Universal Promotion Practices— Nurturing and Responsive Relationships and High-Quality Supportive Environments

In the *Pyramid Model*, building positive relationships with children, families, and colleagues is the foundation for all other practices and the universal conditions that are necessary for promoting social-emotional competence and preventing and addressing challenging behavior. The focus on relationships puts primary importance on the teacher or caregiver engaging in responsive and positive interactions with children and the development of partnerships with families and colleagues. This tier is comprised of teaching practices that have been linked to positive behavior and social-emotional outcomes for children, including joining in children's play, having extended conversations with children, promoting the communicative attempts of children, providing positive descriptive feedback to encourage appropriate behavior, and working with families to use these practices at home and in the community (Birch & Ladd, 1998; Bodrova & Leong, 1998; Cox, 2005; Howes & Hamilton, 1993; Howes & Smith, 1995; Kontos, 1999; Mill & Romano-White, 1999; National Research Council, 2001; Pianta, Steinberg, & Rollins, 1995).

The second category of universal practices linked to promoting the social-emotional competence of all children is the provision of environments and teaching practices that support children's engagement in classroom activities and routines (DeKlyen & Odom,

1989; Frede, Austin, & Lindauer, 1993; Holloway & Reichart-Erickson, 1988; Jolivette, Wehby, Canale, & Massey, 2001; National Research Council, 2001; Peisner-Feinberg et al., 2000). These practices include implementing a developmentally appropriate and balanced schedule of activities and explicitly teaching children about the classroom schedule, structuring transitions, teaching and promoting a small number of classroom rules or behavior expectations, providing clear directions, and providing engaging activities.

Tier 2: Targeted Social-Emotional Supports

In the *Pyramid Model*, the second tier includes the provision of explicit instruction in social skills and emotional competencies (Coie & Koeppl, 1990; Denham & Burton, 1996; Mize & Ladd, 1990; National Research Council, 2001; Schneider, 1974; Serna, Nielsen, Lambros, & Forness, 2000; Shure & Spivack, 1980; Vaughn & Ridley, 1983; Webster-Stratton, Reid, & Hammond, 2001). The objective of the secondary tier of practices is to provide instruction to children who are at risk of developing challenging behavior or who have delays in social-emotional development but for whom more intensive individualized supports might not be necessary. The precise identification of the level of risk is often difficult to discern among young children due to the developmental nature of challenging behavior. Most young children will engage in challenging behavior at some point. Further, many young children are experiencing group care for the first time and have not learned how to navigate social contexts. A primary goal of early childhood education is to teach the social skills and emotional competencies that help children to be successful in group settings. Thus, the *Pyramid Model* includes the instruction of social-emotional skills for all children and the delivery of targeted skill instruction that is individualized and systematic to children who are at risk for having challenges in social interaction or emotional regulation and developing challenging behavior.

Teachers should provide instruction on the following skills: identifying and expressing emotions, self-regulation, social problem solving, initiating and maintaining interactions, cooperative responding, strategies for handling disappointment and anger, and friendship skills (e.g., being helpful, taking turns, giving compliments). In addition, teachers should develop strategies for partnering with families in the instruction of these skills in both the home and preschool settings.

The instruction of social skills and emotional competencies requires a systematic and comprehensive approach using embedded instruction within and across planned and routine activities. Effective teaching strategies include teaching the concept, modeling, rehearsing, role playing, prompting children in context, and providing feedback when the behavior occurs (Grisham-Brown, Hemmeter & Pretti-Frontczak, 2005).

Tier 3: Intensive, Individualized Interventions

The *Pyramid Model* includes the implementation of comprehensive, assessment-based behavior support plans for children with persistent challenging behaviors (Chandler, Dahlquist, Repp, & Feltz, 1999; Dunlap, Wilson, Strain, & Lee, 2013; Fox & Clarke, 2006; Fox, Dunlap, & Cushing, 2002; Reichle et al., 1996). When a child has persistent challenging behavior that is unresponsive to classroom-wide guidance procedures and the instruction of social and emotional skills, a collaborative team, that includes the family, is formed to engage in the process of individualized positive behavior support (I-PBS).

The I-PBS process begins with a team meeting to discuss the child's needs and develop strategies for gathering information through a functional assessment process. The classroom teacher and family contribute to the functional assessment process by providing observation data and participating in interviews. Once functional assessment data have been gathered, the collaborative team meets again to confirm behavior hypotheses and identify potential behavior support strategies. The behavior support plan includes antecedent prevention strategies to address the triggers of challenging behavior, replacement skills that are alternatives to the challenging behavior, and consequence strategies that ensure challenging behavior is not reinforced or maintained. The behavior support plan is designed to address both home and preschool routines where challenging behavior is occurring. In this process, the team also considers supports to the families and strategies to address broader ecological factors that affect the family and their support of the child (e.g., housing, transportation, mental health supports) and issues that may affect the developmental status of the child (e.g., trauma counseling, medical treatment).

Once the behavior support plan is designed, it is implemented by classroom staff and the family. The behavior specialist or consultant provides the teacher with coaching during the initial days of implementation and is available to the family as they implement the behavior support strategies at home and in the community. The teacher and family collect ongoing data, usually in the form of a behavior rating scale, to provide information on the effectiveness of the plan in reducing behavior incidents. The collaborative team meets on a regular basis to review plan implementation and child outcomes.

The TPOT was designed for use in preschool classrooms to evaluate classroomwide implementation of universal and targeted practices associated with the *Pyramid Model*. In addition, the TPOT includes items designed to measure the teacher's capacity to individualize practices and implement individualized behavior support plans. Due to the individualized nature of systematic instruction and individualized behavior support plans, the TPOT is not sufficient for measuring the fidelity with which teachers implement individualized instruction or individualized behavior support plans. Assessing the fidelity of individualized supports will require a more precise measurement based on individualized instructional or behavior support plans (Duda, Dunlap, Fox, Lentini, & Clarke, 2004; Dunlap et al., 2013; Greenwood, 2009; Wolery, 2011).

DEVELOPMENT OF THE TPOT

In 2005, a pilot version of the TPOT was developed and subsequently used in a number of studies (described in Chapters 1 and 7). Based on these studies, the *Teaching Pyramid Observation Tool (TPOT™) for Preschool Classrooms, Research Edition* was developed. In this chapter, we describe the process that was used to develop the pilot version, how the tool was revised based on data from research on the pilot version, and the structure and format of the *TPOT Research Edition*.

Description of the Pilot Version

The development of the pilot version of the TPOT began in 2005. The goal was to develop an efficient and practical instrument that could be used in authentic preschool settings. As part of two federally funded projects (the Center for Evidence Based Practices: Young Children with Challenging Behavior funded by the Office of Special Education Programs and the Center on the Social and Emotional Foundations for Early Learning [CSEFEL] funded by the Department of Health and Human Services), a comprehensive set of training materials was developed for use in professional development activities related to the *Pyramid Model* framework.

The CSEFEL training modules contained an Inventory of Practices that included 130 practices associated with implementing the *Pyramid Model* framework. This inventory was used as one source for key practice indicators included on the pilot version of the

TPOT. The following steps were used to develop key practice items and associated indicators for the pilot version of the TPOT:

1. Generation of a list of potential items that reflected key practice categories (e.g., teaching children to express emotions, promoting children's engagement) based on a thorough review and synthesis of the literature (Dunlap et al., 2006; Joseph & Strain, 2003);

2. Generation of a definition for each key practice category that would become a TPOT item (e.g., teaching children to express emotions, promoting children's engagement) and specification of a list of observable indicators associated with each category (e.g., teacher models or labels own emotions or appropriate ways to express emotions and teacher provides children with strategies to use when they are angry to calm down as observable indicators associated with the key practice item related to teaching children to express emotions);

3. Identification of which practices from the Inventory of Practices should be assigned to which key practice categories as observable indicators;

4. Development of additional categories when practices from the Inventory of Practices did not fit into one of the key categories of practice identified;

5. Development of additional indicators that were identified as important based on reviews of the literature but which did not appear on the Inventory of Practices.

After these steps, further development of the pilot version of the TPOT involved iterative processes of content validation by experts and field testing in authentic preschool settings. All the preceding activities culminated in the pilot version of the instrument. The pilot version of the TPOT had the following structure:

- Fourteen items that represented key practice categories for preschool classrooms associated with the *Pyramid Model* framework with multiple practice indicators associated with each item;
- Seven items related to environmental arrangements in the classroom;
- One item focused on challenging behavior, including whether or not it occurred during a TPOT administration and 10 practice indicators related to strategies teachers use to respond to challenging behavior;
- Sixteen red flags, which represented classroom practices that are inconsistent or incompatible with *Pyramid Model* implementation.

Fourteen items represented key practices (e.g., teaching children to express emotions) and associated observable indicators of the practice that emerged as a result of the categorization (e.g., teacher models or labels own emotions or appropriate ways to express emotions). Specific observable practices were included as indicators under each key practice item. Indicators associated with each TPOT item reflected universal promotion practices, secondary or targeted practices, and the teacher's capacity to individualize practices at the tertiary level.

Seven indicators were included on the pilot version that represented classroom environment variables. These items were scored as either present or absent based on an observation of the classroom. The environmental indicators included practices related to the physical design of and materials in learning centers; the physical arrangement of the classroom; the adequacy of materials; the preparation of teachers related to leading activities; and the quantity, type, and posting of behavioral expectations.

A separate item was included on the pilot version that addressed practices teachers use to respond to children's challenging behavior. This item and the indicators associated with it could only be scored if challenging behavior occurred. First, the observer had to indicate if challenging behavior occurred. Then, if challenging behavior occurred, there were 10 practice indicators that could be scored. The practice indicators were scored based on teacher responses to all incidences of challenging behavior.

Red flags were also included on the pilot version of the TPOT. Red flags are observable practices that either are counterproductive or not supportive of young children's social-emotional skills or are not appropriate prevention or intervention practices for addressing challenging behavior (e.g., teacher reprimands children for expressing their emotions).

Development of the Research Edition

Based on psychometric data for the pilot version of the TPOT and feedback from users, revisions were made, which resulted in the Research Edition of the TPOT. The revisions included structural changes, reorganization of sections, and changes in wording of items and indicators. First, some of the environmental arrangement indicators were included as indicators under key practice items. For example, the environmental arrangement practices related to behavior expectations were integrated into the key practice item on teaching behavior expectations. In some cases, the practices associated with the environmental arrangement indicators were added to the red flags. For example, the environmental indicator focused on teacher preparation for activities was rewritten as a red flag (i.e., teachers are not prepared for activities before children arrive at the activity). Second, the format of the practice indicators within a key practice item was revised. Rather than placing practice indicators under a key practice item anchor score (i.e., 1, 3, 5), the practice indicators are listed in order from easier to implement or universal to more difficult to implement or more targeted or individualized. Third, the wording of indicators that were difficult to score was revised. Fourth, some items were redesigned. Indicators associated with the collaborative teaming item were revised to be scored based on observation only; indicators on the pilot version for this item were scored based on teacher interview. The challenging behavior item was rewritten such that the use of the strategies was scored based on each incident of challenging behavior. Finally, the manual was expanded to include guidance and definitions or clarifications for every indicator associated with each key practice item, for the red flags, and for indicators associated with the challenging behavior item. In Chapter 7, a table shows a side-by-side comparison of the pilot version and the research edition of the TPOT.

Content for the Research Edition of the TPOT has been organized in three subscales: Key Practices; Red Flags; and Responses to Challenging Behavior. In the following sections, we describe each of these subscales and the associated items and indicators.

Key Practices

There are 14 Key Practice items. Each item includes a set of practice indicators that are scored based on observation, interview, or both. Instructions for scoring are included in Chapter 3. In the following section, we describe each key practice item and associated indicators.

Schedules, Routines, and Activities: An important aspect of preschool classrooms is the daily schedule of activities and routines. A well-designed schedule includes a balance of teacher-directed and child-directed activities and large- and small-group activities, minimizes the time children spend in activities in which they are not actively engaged, and is implemented with sufficient consistency so that children can learn the daily schedule. This item includes indicators that address practices related to designing and implementing the schedule, preparing children for changes in the schedule, modifying activities when children lose interest, and providing individual supports to children as needed to engage in classroom activities and routines.

Transitions Between Activities Are Appropriate: This item includes practices designed to increase children's engagement in transitions and decrease the likelihood of challenging behavior occurring during transitions. The practices include providing warnings about upcoming transitions, teaching children about the expectations of the transition, decreasing the amount of time children spend waiting with nothing to do, providing feedback for children during transitions, and providing individualized support as needed.

Teachers Engage in Supportive Conversations with Children: This item focuses on how teachers have conversations with children and respond to the communicative attempts of children in a manner that acknowledges and expands children's communication with adults and peers. Indicators for this item reflect the quality of conversations that teachers have with children, the strategies that teachers use to expand children's communication and interactions, and the support teachers provide to individual children in their communication.

Promoting Children's Engagement: Children's active engagement in activities and with peers and adults is critical to early learning. Moreover, children who are actively engaged are less likely to have challenging behavior. When children lose interest in an activity, when an activity is too long, or when children do not understand task or activity demands, they are less likely to be engaged and more likely to exhibit behaviors that disrupt the activity, the teacher, or other children (e.g., crying, hitting other children, leaving the group). Indicators for this item include strategies teachers use to structure activities and interactions to promote the active engagement of all children in the classroom, including strategies that might be used when children have difficulty maintaining engagement.

Providing Directions: The ways teachers provide directions to children can be pivotal to children's ability to understand and respond to directions. When teachers provide directions that are understandable and clear and that tell children what to do, children are more likely to respond appropriately. Indicators for this item address how directions are stated, when directions are provided, and how to support children's understanding of directions.

Collaborative Teaming: The goal of teaming is for the classroom to operate as a well-oiled machine with all adults knowing what to do, engaging with children, and working together. In addition, the tone of the classroom and interactions between staff should be positive. Indicators for this item include how adults talk to each other, the quality of interactions between adults and children, the engagement of all team members in teaching interactions, and the support adults provide to each other.

Teaching Behavior Expectations: The use of behavior expectations (e.g., use soft touches, help your friends, be safe) is a proactive way of addressing behavior by focusing on what children are expected to do rather than simply responding to challenging behavior when it occurs. For example, for a child who hits others when he wants them to play, the teacher can redirect him to use an appropriate behavior by stating a behavior expectation (e.g., "We use our words to ask our friends to play"). Expectations specify appropriate behaviors and focus adults on teaching and supporting the use of these behaviors throughout the day. The indicators include posting the expectations, teaching the expectations, providing feedback to children about their use of the expectations, and helping children to reflect on their use of the expectations.

Teaching Social Skills and Emotional Competencies: This item is one of four items that focuses on teaching specific social skills or emotional competencies. We wanted to measure teachers' use of practices for teaching a range of social skills and emotional competencies including friendship skills, expressing emotions, and problem solving. It was unlikely, however, that a teacher would systematically teach all of these skills in a single 2-hour observation. Thus, we decided to include one item (Teaching Social Skills and Emotional Competencies) that could be scored during an observation and for which the teacher would receive credit for teaching skills from any social-emotional domain (i.e., friendship skills, emotional literacy, problem solving). This item includes practices related to when and how the teacher teaches social skills and emotional competencies, the provision of feedback related to social skills and emotional competencies, and how the teacher individualizes instruction related to these skills. The three additional items on teaching social skills and emotional competencies (described below) each focus on a specific social-emotional domain and can be scored based on observation or interview.

Teaching Friendship Skills: Many challenging behaviors occur in preschool classrooms because of young children's limited experiences in group settings. Young children need support in learning to interact with other children, organize play, request materials, and work together. The indicators reflect practices related to structuring activities to promote interactions between children, teaching friendship skills (e.g., helping each other, taking turns, suggesting play ideas), commenting on children who are engaging in friendship skills, providing individualized support, and teachers modeling, through their own behaviors, friendship skills they expect from children.

Teaching Children to Express Emotions: Young children experience a range of emotions such as sadness, happiness, jealousy, pride, excitement, frustration, and anger. These emotions often result in challenging behavior because children do not know how to express emotions in appropriate ways. For example, a child who is frustrated because he cannot get a box open might throw it on the floor or a child who is angry because a peer has a toy she wants might hit the peer. This item focuses on how teachers help children learn to communicate their emotions in appropriate ways (e.g., ask for help rather than throwing the toy on the floor; using words to tell the teacher or peer she is mad). The indicators reflect practices such as teaching emotions, modeling emotions, commenting on emotions, and providing individualized support to children around emotional expression.

Teaching Problem Solving: In a preschool classroom, social problems often occur (e.g., two children wanting the same toy, a child not wanting another child to interfere with their play). Social problem solving is a complex process that involves children being able to identify a problem, think about possible solutions, evaluate whether those solutions would be appropriate, and use an acceptable and effective solution. The indicators for this item relate to teaching the steps of a social problem-solving process, providing feedback to and commenting on children who are using the problem-solving process, modeling the steps of the process in their actions with children, assisting children in reflecting on their use of problem solving, and providing individualized problem-solving support to children who need it.

Interventions for Children with Persistent Challenging Behavior: The third tier of the *Pyramid Model* involves a process for developing individualized interventions for children with the most persistent and severe challenging behavior. This is a team-based process facilitated by an individual with expertise in behavior support. The teacher's role in the process includes collecting data, participating in the development of the behavior support plan, implementing the strategies in the classroom, and assisting in monitoring the implementation and outcomes of the plan. The indicators for this item relate to each of these activities and are scored based on the teacher's report of participation in these activities.

Connecting with Families: The universal level of the *Pyramid Model* includes a focus on relationships between teachers and children and between teachers and families. Connecting with families is important in terms of building a relationship in which families trust the teacher and are willing to work collaboratively with the teacher to support their children. The practice indicators focus on how the teacher communicates with families, supports family involvement in the classroom and in the child's education, and encourages communication and input from the family.

Supporting Family Use of *Pyramid Model* Practices: At all levels of the *Pyramid Model*, there is an important role for families in terms of promoting their children's social-emotional development and preventing and addressing challenging behavior. Many of the prevention and promotion practices that are described above are relevant for families (e.g., consistency and predictability of routines, teaching children expectations, preparing children for transitions) and need to be communicated to families in ways that translate that information into strategies families can use at home and in the community. Further, families should be involved in the process of developing and implementing individualized behavior support plans. The indicators for this item focus on how teachers provide information to families, work with families to identify their needs, and involve families in developing individualized supports for their children.

Red Flags

Red flags include practices that reflect poor structural (e.g., learning centers do not have clear boundaries; large, wide-open spaces in the classroom where children can run) or process environmental quality (e.g., transitions are more often chaotic than not; the teacher rarely encourages interactions between children during play or activities), or negative climate (e.g., the teacher reprimands or admonishes children for expressing their emotions; children are threatened with an impending negative consequence that will occur if disruptive or challenging behavior persists). Red flags often are associated with incidences of challenging behavior and poor learning outcomes for children.

Using Effective Strategies to Respond to Challenging Behavior

This one-item subscale includes three indicators that represent essential strategies for responding to challenging behavior that have been identified as evidence-based strategies in the literature (e.g., Dunlap, Wilson, Strain, & Lee, 2013). This item does not address prevention strategies (e.g., providing positive feedback for appropriate behavior, providing individualized support to engage) or strategies for teaching replacement skills (e.g., teacher individualizes instruction of social skills) as those practices are represented as indicators under the key practice items. In responding to challenging behavior, it is important that teachers do not engage in actions that escalate or maintain the behavior (e.g., giving high rates of attention to inappropriate attention-seeking behavior), and use developmentally appropriate strategies (e.g., redirection, planned ignoring). As soon as the child behaves appropriately, teachers provide positive attention and feedback about child engagement or appropriate behavior.

SUMMARY

In this chapter, we provided background information about the *Pyramid Model*, described the procedures used to develop the TPOT, and provided an overview of the structure of the TPOT. In addition, we provided a description of the practices reflected on the TPOT. The next chapter describes how to administer the TPOT, including procedures for conducting an observation and the interview, and provides key definitions needed to score the TPOT.

CHAPTER 3

Using the Teaching Pyramid Observation Tool

In this chapter, the procedures for administering the TPOT are described, including how to prepare for the administration of the TPOT, procedures to use during the observation and interview, how to identify incidents of challenging behavior, how to score items, and the training needed prior to using the TPOT. Definitions of key terms are presented at the end of this chapter.

The TPOT is completed based on a 2-hour observation of a preschool classroom and a 15- to 20-minute interview with the teacher. The TPOT observation and interview should be scheduled on the same day, if possible. The TPOT observation should include both teacher-directed (e.g., circle time, small groups) and child-directed (e.g., free play, center time) activities as well as the transitions between activities. The observation should not include meals (e.g., lunch, snack), outdoor play, or other occasions when the entire class is engaged in another type of activity outside of the classroom (e.g., music class).

ARRANGING FOR A TPOT ADMINISTRATION

When planning the TPOT administration with the teacher, it is helpful to ask for the classroom daily schedule. You should let the teacher know about the types of activities you will observe and the need for a short interview during a time that the teacher is not interacting with children. The TPOT is designed to measure implementation of *Pyramid Model* practices that are used by the lead teacher and classroom teaching team. Thus, you should conduct the observation on a day when the lead teacher is present in the classroom and the typical schedule is being followed (e.g., no special visitors, no field trips).

PREPARING FOR YOUR OBSERVATION

Observers should review the TPOT manual and scoring form carefully before conducting the observation and interview. Observers should take the TPOT manual with them to the observation so they can reference it after the observation and interview are completed. Observers should take the scoring form and a pad of paper for recording additional notes while conducting observations in the classroom or when conducting the interview. However, TPOT indicators should not be scored during the observation or interview.

Prior to starting the observation, you should complete the opening page of the TPOT scoring form, indicating the following:

1. Date of the administration

2. Lead teacher name or identification code

3. Observer name or identification code

4. Start time of the observation

5. The number of children and adults present in the classroom

In addition, you should ask the teacher the following questions and record the responses. These questions *must* be asked before beginning the observation because they focus on the children who are present in the classroom for your observation and the scoring of indicators related to individualizing for children:

1. "Are there any children present today who are unable to communicate with you in the same way as other children in the class because they have a severe language delay?"

2. "Are there any children present today who need information presented to them in a different way because they are dual-language learners?"

Figure 3.1 shows a sample opening scoring sheet that has been completed prior to an observation.

Teaching Pyramid Observation Tool (TPOT™) for Preschool Classrooms RESEARCH EDITION ▲TPOT

Date: 3/31/2013   Start time: 8:15 a.m.

Teacher ID: Beth   End time: 11:15 a.m.

Observer ID: Vanessa

Please note if the observation is interrupted or stopped because the majority of children leave the classroom (e.g., to go outside) or are engaged in an activity or routine that is not observed (e.g., snack). If that occurs, indicate the time you stopped the observation, the time the observation was resumed, and the length of time the observation was suspended.

Time observation stopped: 10:00 a.m.   Time observation resumed: 10:30 a.m.

Length of time (in minutes) that observation was suspended: 30 minutes

Notes, *if applicable:* Observation was suspended when the class went to the playground.

Number of adults in classroom:

    at beginning of observation 3   at the end of observation 3

Number of children in classroom:

    at beginning of observation 15   at the end of observation 16

Number of adults who entered room at some point during observation: 2

To most effectively answer SC10 if the observer is not familiar with the classroom, he or she should ask the teacher the following questions and record the responses PRIOR TO THE OBSERVATION:

"Are there any children present today who are unable to communicate with you in
the same way as other children in the class because they have a severe language delay?"   ☒ Yes   ☐ No

"Are there any children present today who need information presented to them in
a different way because they are dual-language learners?"   ☒ Yes   ☐ No

NOTES:

Figure 3.1. Sample opening page of the scoring form.

DURING THE OBSERVATION

While conducting the TPOT observation, observers should position themselves in a location where they can view the activities of the teacher. Observers should refrain from interacting with children and should not join classroom activities. Your goal is to be as unobtrusive as possible and to minimize any disruption that might result from your presence in the classroom.

The TPOT scoring form is used during the observation to record observation notes. Scoring does not occur until after the observation and interview are completed. We have found the most effective way to conduct an observation is for the observer to focus on what the teachers are doing (versus watching children) and keep a running record of notes about actions of the teacher that are related to the implementation of the *Pyramid Model* practices. Observers should refrain from scoring TPOT indicators while conducting their observation.

The scoring form includes a page to record the schedule of classroom activities that are observed. Use this page to note each type of activity observed (e.g., circle/ teacher-directed, centers/child-initiated, small group, and transitions), the approximate start time and end time of each activity, the total number of minutes for each activity, and any relevant notes. These notes will be helpful when scoring several TPOT indicators related to the schedule and activities (e.g., balance of child-directed and teacher-directed activities). There is also a space on the scoring form to note if you stop the observation (and for how long) because the teacher or children leave the room (e.g., to go to playground or recess) or engage in an activity that will not be observed (e.g., meals). Indicate the time you stopped the observation, the time the observation was resumed, and the length of time the observation was suspended. See Figure 3.2 for a sample page of the scoring form completed during an observation.

To score the items, the observer should consider the actions of the lead teacher because she or he is typically responsible for the teaching approach and teaching practices used with children, the structure and pacing of classroom activities, and the other members of the teaching team. Generally, indicators will be scored based on the behavior of all adults in the classroom. However, when there is a discrepancy between the behavior of the lead teacher and the behavior of other staff, the indicator should be scored based on the lead teacher's behavior (e.g., if the lead teacher's tone in conversations with children is primarily negative and the assistant's tone is positive, you would score the indicator based on the lead teacher's behavior). When scoring red flags, the scoring should consider the behavior of all adults in the classroom. Thus, the observer should score any action by any adult in the classroom that is a red flag, regardless of who is observed using the red flag practices. For the challenging behavior item, the observer should score the behavior of the adult who intervenes with a child who has an incident of challenging behavior. Additional information about scoring is described later in this chapter.

ENDING THE OBSERVATION

When you have completed your observation, you should note (a) the number of children and adults in the classroom at the end of the observation, (b) the number of adults who entered the room at some point during the observation, and (c) the time the observation ended.

CONDUCTING THE INTERVIEW

The interview should be conducted with the lead teacher during a time the teacher identifies she can be away from the children. The interview typically lasts 15 to 20 minutes and

SCHEDULE OF ACTIVITIES   ▲TPOT

The grid below provides a place for you to write down activities as they occur and the time spent in each activity.

ACTIVITY	START TIME	END TIME	TOTAL # MINUTES	NOTES
Free play	8:15	8:30	15	Children were arriving
Transition	8:30	8:40	10	
Morning meeting	8:40	9:00	20	
Transition	9:00	9:05	5	
Centers	9:05	9:45	40	
Transition	9:45	10:00	15	
Outside play	10:00	10:30	30	
Transition	10:30	10:35	5	Class came in from outside play
Large group	10:35	10:45	10	

Figure 3.2. Sample schedule page of the scoring form.

should be completed on the same day as the observation. The observer should ask the questions exactly as stated in the scoring form. The scoring form also provides a script for clarifying a question if the teacher appears confused or unable to answer the question when initially posed.

When conducting the interview, teachers who are unfamiliar with the *Pyramid Model* might appear to be at a loss for how to answer a question. Observers should record the answer the teacher provides and acknowledge the response (e.g., nod head, make notes) and then move on to the next question. During the interview, the observer should write down everything the teacher says and later use those responses to score the indicators associated with items that are scored by interview or by interview and observation.

SCORING THE TPOT

The TPOT is scored after the observation and interview are completed. Notes recorded during the observation and interview will guide the observer in determining the scores for each indicator. It is important to do the scoring immediately after conducting the TPOT. If there are circumstances that delay the interview portion to the following day, the observation-only items (Items 1–8) should be scored on the same day the observation is completed.

Items Scored Based on Observation Only

For Items 1–8, the scoring of indicators will be based solely on the observation conducted in the classroom. When scoring the indicators for Items 1–8, the observer will check *Yes* or *No* for each indicator based on the observation (see Figure 3.3 for a sample item and indicators). In addition, there are four indicators (SR8, SC10, ENG8, CT4) for which *N/O* (no opportunity to observe) can be scored. Indicators associated with Item 6, collaborative teaming, measure the extent to which classroom staff work together as a team. If there is only one staff member (teacher) in the classroom, omit that item and do not score any of the indicators associated with the item.

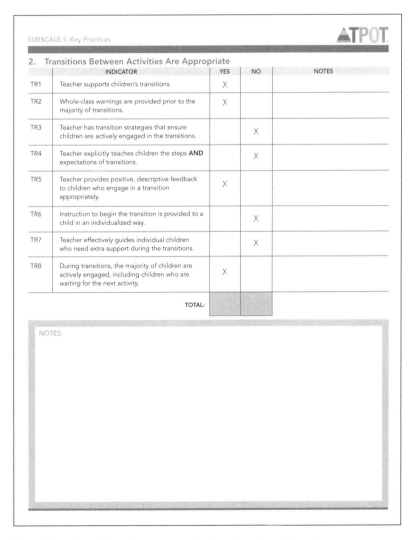

Figure 3.3. A sample item that was completed based on observation only.

Items Scored Based on Both Observation and Interview

The scoring of indicators associated with Items 9–11 will be based on both the observation and the interview (see Figure 3.4 for a sample item with indicators completed based on both observation and interview). For each indicator associated with Items 9–11, check *Yes* or *No*. When marking an indicator associated with Items 9–11 as *Yes*, you must also mark *R* (reported), *O* (observed), or both. When scoring an indicator associated with Items 9–11 as *No*, it is not necessary to mark *R* or *O*.

It is possible that a teacher might report implementing a practice and the practice is not observed in the classroom or the practice is observed but not reported by the teacher. Below are decision rules about how to score indicators that include *O* and *R:*

- If you observe the practice associated with the indicator but the teacher does not report the practice in the interview, mark *Yes* and indicate that the practice was observed *(O).*

- If the teacher reports that the practice is used and you see the practice used, mark *Yes* and indicate that the practice was observed *(O)* and reported *(R).*

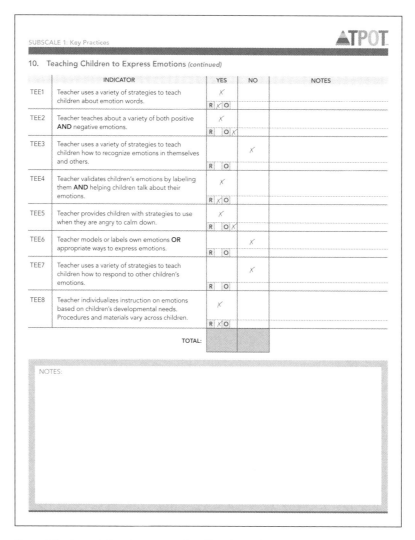

Figure 3.4.   A sample item that was completed based on both observation and interview.

- If the teacher does not report use of the practice and you do not see the practice used, mark *No.*
- If the teacher reports the use of a practice but you did not observe the teacher using the practice as reported, mark *No.*
- If the teacher reports the use of a practice but you observe the use of a practice that is counter to what the teacher reported (e.g., you observed a teacher reprimand a child about expressing emotions, but the teacher reported always validating children's emotions), mark *No.*
- If the teacher reports the use of a practice and there is no opportunity to use the practice during the observation, mark *Yes* and reported *(R).*

Items Scored Based on Interview Only

The scoring of indicators associated with Items 12–14 are based on the interview only (see Figure 3.5 for a sample item completed based on interview only). For each indicator

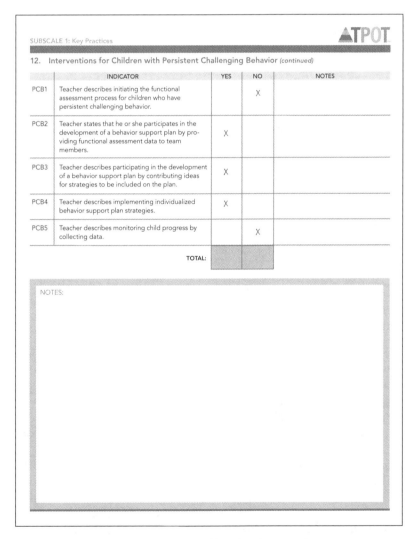

Figure 3.5. A sample item that was completed based on interview only.

associated with Items 12–14, you will check *Yes* or *No*. It is possible that the teacher's response to an interview question will address an indicator other than the one for which the interview question is designed. If this occurs, the response can be used to score the relevant indicator.

Red Flags

Red flags (Items 15–28) are scored based on whether or not you observe them in the classroom during the observation portion of the TPOT administration. These items provide information to guide teacher training and support or to inform program policies and procedures. Red Flags 29 (teacher reports asking for removal of children with persistent challenging behavior from the classroom or program) and 31 (teacher restrains a child when engaging in problem behavior or secludes the child in an area separate from the classroom where the child cannot see the activities of the classroom) are scored based on the teacher's responses to interview questions from Item 12 (interventions for children with persistent challenging behavior) or based on actions of staff noted during the observation portion of the TPOT administration. Red Flag 30 (teacher makes comments about families that are focused on the challenges presented by families and their lack of interest in being involved) is scored based on the teacher's responses to interview questions from Items 13 (connecting with families) and 14 (supporting family use of *Pyramid Model* practices).

Challenging Behavior Item

This item and the indicators associated with it are only scored when challenging behavior occurs. The item is scored for each incident of challenging behavior that occurs during the observation. For each incident, the observer must first determine if the observed challenging behavior meets the following definition:

> Challenging behavior is defined as behavior that includes 1) physical aggression, such as hitting, kicking, punching, spitting, throwing objects forcefully, pinching, pushing, and biting; 2) climbing on things in the classroom that are not permitted; 3) destroying property, destroying what another child is working on regardless of the other child's response; 4) taking toys away from other children forcefully; 5) running that poses a safety risk for the child or others or elopement from the classroom; 6) tantrum behaviors that might include behaviors such as kicking, screaming, pushing an object or person, stomping feet, or head banging; 7) verbal aggression including yelling, threats, screaming at another person, calling children bad names, and saying bad words; 8) ordering an adult to do something (e.g., "leave me alone"); 9) persistent or prolonged crying that is loud or disruptive or ongoing crying that interferes with the child's engagement in activities; 10) inappropriate use of materials (e.g., jumping off chairs, slamming materials, throwing objects); 11) statements that are noncompliant (e.g., "I'm not going to do it") or clear and explicit verbal or physical refusal to follow directions; or 12) inappropriate touching, stripping, and other behaviors that are hurtful, disruptive, or dangerous to self or others.

An incident might occur during an activity where the challenging behavior is characterized by its duration (e.g., persistent and prolonged crying) versus an event or single action (e.g., hit, refusal to follow directions). To determine how to identify and segment incidents for coding, note if it is one action versus a duration behavior (e.g., cries off and on throughout circle). Examples of what might be segmented and coded as a single incident of challenging behavior include the following: hits child to get toy (single action) or yells

"You're stupid" to a teacher (single action). For duration behaviors (e.g., persistent crying), segment the incident by activity. For example, if a child cries off and on throughout circle, record it as one incident and score the indicators based on what the teacher does or does not do for the duration of the behavior. If the crying continues during a subsequent transition, record it as a separate incident. If a different challenging behavior occurs by the same child during the activity that the crying is occurring (e.g., hitting an adult), score that as a separate incident.

There is a place on the scoring form to indicate information related to each incident that meets the definition for challenging behavior. On the scoring form, a note is entered to provide a brief description of the incident (e.g., child cried persistently during circle). Once you determine that the behavior incident meets the definition, you should watch the adult who responds to the child during the incident and note the strategies used. There are two sets of practice indicators to observe: essential strategies and additional strategies. For each incident, the observer watches to determine if any of the three essential strategies were used by the adult. The observer should score *Yes* or *No* for each of the three essential strategies used by the adult for each incident of challenging behavior that occurred during the observation. This scoring is repeated for every incident observed. After the observation is complete, the observer should also record if any of the additional strategies were used by the teacher in response to any of the behavior incidents. The observer should score *Yes* for all of the additional strategies that the adults were observed to use in response to any of the incidents of challenging behavior that occurred during the observation. The checklist of additional strategies will be used for coaching teachers but will not factor into the score for this item.

The score for the challenging behavior item is determined in the following manner:

1. If no incidents of challenging behavior were observed, indicate *no incidents observed* for the item. No other score is needed.

2. If incidents of challenging behavior occurred and all essential strategies were observed in response to all incidents, score *Yes* for the item.

3. If incidents of challenging behavior occurred but only some of the essential strategies were used in response to some of the incidents or all three of the essential strategies were used in response to only some of the incidents, score *No* for the item.

When an incident occurs that meets the definition of challenging behavior but the child is taken out of the classroom, do not leave the classroom to continue to observe the strategies used by the staff. You should record that an incident of challenging behavior occurred but would not score the indicators for the challenging behavior item. Make a note on the score form that the child was taken out of the classroom so you were not able to observe how staff responded to challenging behavior. Similarly, if an incident occurs and you are unable to see the adult response to the behavior incident within the classroom, make a note that the incident occurred and you were unable to observe the response.

RECOMMENDED TRAINING PROCEDURES BEFORE USING THE TPOT

The TPOT is a comprehensive measure of teaching practices that requires training for reliable use. We strongly recommend individuals or groups from programs or agencies who want to use the TPOT participate in training from an individual who has been identified as a TPOT Approved Trainer by the authors or publisher. Before participating in TPOT training, we recommend participation in professional development activities focused on the *Pyramid Model* and implementation of *Pyramid Model* practices in preschool classrooms. Users should have a thorough understanding of the *Pyramid Model* and the practices associated with the model prior to being trained to use the TPOT.

A typical TPOT training lasts 1.5 to 2 days. On the first day, the training includes a review of the manual, training on each of the items and the scoring guidance for associated indicators, and procedures to use when conducting the observation and interview. Participants practice observing and scoring items using short video clips and complete their training by scoring at least one 2-hour videotaped observation and subsequent interview. Participants' scores on the full-length videotaped TPOT are compared to a master code to determine if the minimum of 80% agreement on key practice indicators and red flags is reached. For the challenging behavior item, we recommend users have 80% or greater agreement about the number of incidents of challenging behavior that occur during the observation and 100% agreement about the three essential strategies used for each incident of challenging behavior scored by both observers. If the criterion described above is not achieved, the participant scores an additional videotape.

In addition to using videotapes to assess agreement with consensus scores, we recommend users administer the TPOT at least three times in preschool classrooms and evaluate their scores against another trained TPOT observer before administering the TPOT independently. Total score agreement across all scored indicators for Key Practice items, Red Flags, and the summary score for Responses to Challenging Behavior should meet or exceed 80% across the three practice administrations. If the TPOT is being used regularly to assess teacher implementation fidelity or to guide professional development efforts, we recommend that periodic interrater agreement checks are used to ensure that observers are using the tool reliably.

KEY DEFINITIONS IN THE TPOT

The following terms appear in the TPOT indicators and scoring guidance. Definitions for how these terms are used within the TPOT are provided below. Observers should review these definitions prior to conducting the TPOT so that interpretation of these terms is consistent with the interpretation of the TPOT authors.

Child-directed activity: A child-directed activity is a learning experience that occurs in a preschool classroom that allows frequent opportunities for child choice and expression. Examples of child-directed activities include free choice, center time, or other activities that the child chooses to do and completes using materials they choose.

Directions: Directions refer to explicit verbal or nonverbal guidelines or instructions given by an adult related to desired child action(s).

Dual-language learner (DLL): Dual-language learner is a term used to describe children who are learning two (or more) languages. One language they are learning is often English.

Engagement: Engagement refers to a child's active attending or participation in an activity. For example, a child is considered engaged when he or she is following directions, actively communicating or interacting with a peer or adult, or manipulating or using materials relevant to the activity or task. Some children served in preschool classrooms might have behaviors that appear to be incompatible with engagement, such as stereotypic behaviors (e.g., humming, hand flapping, rocking) or not making direct eye contact (e.g., looks from the side). When these types of behaviors are present, do *not* make the assumption that the child is not engaged. The interpretation of whether a child is engaged should be made based on your observation that the child is attending or participating in the activity or interaction, even when stereotypic behaviors are also occurring (e.g., a child might be flapping his hands but is still facing and listening to the teacher who is reading a book).

Emotional competencies: Emotional competencies refer to behaviors related to emotion expression, emotion understanding, and emotion regulation (e.g., telling a friend you are sad, helping a child who is hurt, walking away when mad).

Functional assessment: Functional assessment is a systematic, team-based process for determining the function of a child's challenging behavior in order to develop and implement a plan to address the challenging behavior.

Large-group activity: Large-group activities are defined as teacher-guided learning experiences that involve all or almost all children in the classroom.

Logical consequences: Logical consequences are actions or responses of an adult that occur after a child's challenging behavior that are clearly related to the child's challenging behavior. These actions or responses are intended to discourage escalation or additional occurrences of the challenging behavior. For example, the teacher might say, "If you can't share the truck by taking turns, we will have to put it away," and then removes the truck when the child continues to argue over possession of the truck or refuses to share.

Positive descriptive feedback: Positive descriptive feedback refers to a teacher providing positive feedback to a child using words that describe the behavior for which the child is being acknowledged. For example, if a child is sitting in a chair at a circle activity in a manner consistent with teacher or classroom expectations, instead of the teacher saying, "Good job!" to the child, the teacher says, "Thank you for sitting in your chair with your feet on the floor!" Other examples include the following: "When you heard the clean-up song, you started cleaning up right away" and "I can tell you are ready because your eyes are on me, you are sitting on your name, and your voice is quiet."

Problem solving: Problem solving refers to children's use of skills that help them address problems encountered in social situations (e.g., peer conflicts, unable to get needs or wants addressed). The steps of social problem solving include identifying the problem, thinking about possible solutions, considering what the outcomes of these solutions may be, trying a solution, and evaluating how the solution worked for solving the problem.

Routines: Routines are predictable activities that focus on eating, self-care, or physical activity. Examples of routines that might be observed during a TPOT observation include arrival routines (e.g., hanging up a coat, putting lunch box away), getting a drink, and washing hands.

Small-group activities: Small-group activities are defined as teacher-guided learning experiences in which children are asked to engage with materials or in activities or instruction that is planned, focused on specific content, and directed by a teacher or other staff member.

Social skills: Social skills refer to behaviors observed when children interact with peers and adults (e.g., initiating, responding, organizing play, greeting, helping a friend, taking turns, offering solutions to common social problems).

Teacher: The teacher is any adult in a classroom who is involved in teaching or supporting children's learning. This can include lead teachers, teaching assistants, or therapists who are engaged in activities with children within the classroom.

Teacher-directed activity: A teacher-directed activity is a learning experience structured and led by the teacher, which has limited opportunities for child choice or free expression. Large-group activities led by a teacher, small-group activities led by a teacher, and one-to-one instruction during which a teacher conducts instructional trials are considered teacher-directed activities.

Transition: A transition is the physical movement of children in the classroom from one activity to another. This can occur in a staggered fashion (small groups of children moving or one child moving), but it eventually results in the movement of the majority of children from one activity to another.

Transition warning: A transition warning refers to a signal or verbal reminder that an activity will be starting or ending. A transition warning might be a verbal statement (e.g., "We will clean up in 5 minutes"), or a nonverbal signal or cue (e.g., turning the classroom lights on and off) or a song.

Visuals: Visuals are supports a teacher displays to help children understand a concept, behavior expectation, or printed text. Visuals include, but are not limited to, pictures, line drawings, photographs, and magazine clippings. For example, the teacher might have photographs on the shelves to show children where toys go, a classroom schedule that includes photographs, or a choice board with photographs.

SUMMARY

In this chapter, we provided guidance on how to administer the TPOT, including conducting both the observation and the interview. We provided information about the different types of TPOT items and showed some examples of how to use the scoring form. In addition, we described how users should be trained and procedures that should be used to ensure they meet or exceed interrater agreement standards. Finally, we provided definitions for key terms. In the next chapter, we provide the scoring guidance, rules, and definitions for the TPOT.

CHAPTER 4

Teaching Pyramid Observation Tool Scoring Guidance

In this chapter, we provide scoring guidance for the TPOT. This guidance must be used to determine if the observed or reported practices can be scored as occurring in the classroom.

Item 1. Schedules, Routines, and Activities

SR1. A classroom schedule is displayed on the wall that provides information on the sequence of daily activities. The schedule does not have to be posted at child's eye level or include visuals to score *Yes* for SR1.

SR2. The schedule must be posted so that children can see the schedule (at eye level) and visuals (pictures, line drawings, or photographs) must be included on the posted schedule. If the posted schedule does not meet these criteria, you must also score *No* on items SR5 and SR8.

SR3. Score *Yes* for SR3 if the duration of each teacher-directed activity is 20 minutes or less. This includes situations when two back-to-back structured small-group activities occur and each is less than 20 minutes, provided children are given an opportunity to move around between each small-group activity (e.g., by physically moving to a new small-group activity location or stretching or changing positions before starting a new small-group activity in the same location). If more than two back-to-back structured small-group activities are offered within a 40- to 45-minute timeframe, only score *Yes* for SR3 if each activity is 20 minutes or less in duration and children are not required to participate in more than two of the activities. Examples of teacher-directed activities are large-group activities, structured small-group activities, or structured one-to-one instruction. If the activity is initiated and guided by the teacher, it is a teacher-directed activity. A small-group art lesson that requires the children to follow a set of steps to create a final product is a teacher-directed activity. An example of an activity that would not be characterized as teacher directed is children choosing to make a picture in the art center during free-choice time, determining the materials they will use to make the picture, and determining the subject of the picture. The teacher could engage children in conversation about the process of making the picture and the subject of the picture, and the activity would still be a child-directed activity. The teacher joining in children's play and embedding skill instruction in play is not a teacher-directed activity. Activities such as snack time and toileting are considered routines, not teacher-directed or child-directed activities. *Routines should not be taken into consideration when scoring this indicator.*

SR4. To score *Yes*, you must observe both small-group activities and large-group activities during the observation. Small-group activities are teacher-guided activities in which

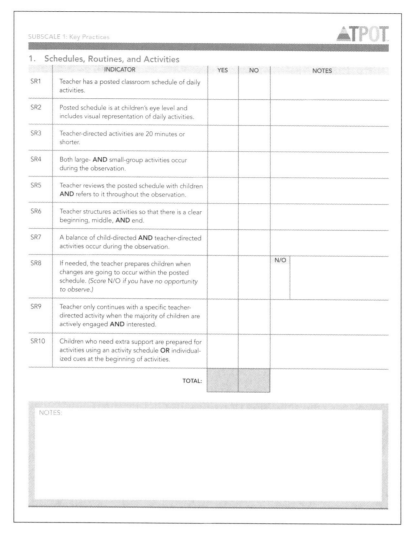

Item 1. Schedules, Routines, and Activities

children are engaged with materials, activities, or instruction and that are planned and focused on specific content. Small-group activities can occur during center time if the adult directs a small group of children as described in the previous sentence. However, when adults interact with children in small groups during center and there is not a planned activity, it is not considered small group.

SR5. To score *Yes*, the teacher reviews all or part of the posted schedule with the class as appropriate, and this must happen multiple times during the observation. *Yes* can also be scored if teacher reviews the schedule verbally multiple times during the observation, although a visual schedule should also be posted.

SR6. To score *Yes*, the activity should have a clear beginning, middle, and end (i.e., children generally know what to expect as part of the activity or it appears from the observation that the activity has a logical progression or flow). An example of an activity that has a clear beginning, middle, or end is circle time that begins with an opening song, includes several activities, and ends with a closing song, ritual, or transition. However, if no strategy was used to let children know that circle time was starting, the teacher did not seem to have a planned sequence for activities while at circle, or there was no indication that the circle ended before the next major activity started, then the activity did not have a clear beginning, middle, and end.

SR7. In order to score *Yes* on this indicator, both child- and teacher-directed activities must be observed during the 2-hour observation period, with child-directed activities taking place for at least 50% of the observation time. Routines should not be taken into consideration when scoring this indicator. During centers, consider what the majority of the children are doing. If the majority of children are engaged in child-directed activities, then this time should be considered child directed. If, however, most of the children are engaged in teacher-directed activities and only some children are engaged in free choice during centers, then this time would be counted as teacher-directed time. If 50% or more of the children are in child-directed activities, score the activity as child directed.

SR8. To score *Yes*, the teacher should use or refer to the posted schedule to indicate to children that an activity will be changed. For example, the teacher might put a universal *no* symbol over an activity or remove a visual of an activity such as outdoor play and replace it with a symbol for a cooking project to indicate that outdoor play will not occur. Other examples of changes would be going on a field trip or not being able to go outside because of weather. Score *N/O* (no opportunity) if there are no changes in the posted schedule when observing. *If item SR5 is scored* No, *this item also must be scored as* No.

SR9. The purpose of this item is to determine if teachers modify activities when children are not engaged or become disinterested in an activity. The teacher should change or end the activity if more than 25% of children are not engaged. If 75% or more of the children are engaged, assume the teacher is modifying the lesson based on children's engagement and interests. For additional information, refer to the definition of engagement provided in Chapter 3.

SR10. If children who clearly need a visual schedule or cue are not given one during the observation, score this item as *No*. The activity schedule might be used or a cue might be given before the group direction or immediately following the group direction. A child may need a schedule or cue if he or she appears confused about what is happening; the child wanders around at the start of an activity; the child has a "meltdown" when transitions occur; the child stands still, looking aimlessly around the room for a prolonged period of time at the start of an activity; or the child does not transition to a new activity. If all children are engaged in the beginning of the scheduled activities in the manner intended, then assume all children are receiving the level of support they need and score *Yes*.

Item 2. Transitions between Activities are Appropriate

TR1. To score *Yes*, the teacher should support children by letting them know what to do during transitions. For example, the teacher might say, "Clean up the center area that you are in" or "Find a partner and come to circle."

TR2. To score *Yes*, a whole-class warning must be provided for the majority of transitions. A whole-class warning is a prompt delivered in advance about the upcoming transition that occurs at least 1 minute prior to the transition. This could be a verbal statement, song, movement, or other signal or cue.

TR3. Transition strategies may include songs, games, or helping children plan for the next activity. For example, the teacher might say the transition warning, "It's time to go to centers," and then ask each child a question before she sends them to the next activity. During this time, children may be waiting to take their turn to answer a question. In this situation, the teacher would get credit for TR3.

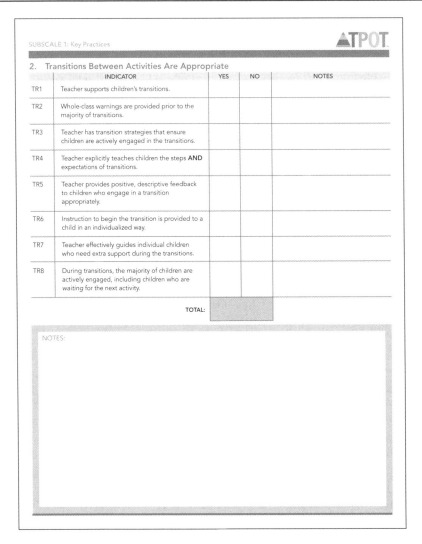

Item 2. Transitions Between Activities are Appropriate

TR4. Score *Yes* for this item when the teacher describes what the children should do during the transition. For example, the teacher may say, "Before you go outside, stop at your cubby and get your coat and your glasses" or "We are going to centers. When I call your name, you can put your mat away, get your name, and choose a center." Depending on the time of year that the observation takes place, explicit teaching of the transition steps or expectations might not occur if the children have already learned the expectations for the transition. If the transitions in the class run smoothly and the children are engaged and appear to know what to do, it can be assumed that explicit teaching about transitions has happened at some point; therefore, this indicator can be scored as *Yes*. If the teacher provides instructions about the transition and then begins a different activity before transitioning, the instructions would not count and you would score *No* for this indicator unless the teacher gave new instructions immediately prior to the transition. You would also score *No* for this indicator if the only instruction the teacher gives related to the transition is to be quiet and listen to the instructions.

TR5. An example of positive, descriptive feedback during a transition is when the teacher says, "You cleaned up after snack all by yourself," rather than just saying, "Good job!" To score *Yes*, this feedback should be provided during the majority of the transitions.

TR6. To score *Yes*, a whole-class direction for the transition must be given and additional instruction, directions, or support must be given to an individual child. An individual child is provided with instruction or support *to begin* a transition in a manner that is different or supplemental to the whole-class direction. This might be in the form of additional instructions, reminders, gestures, assistance, visuals, or other supports. If all children transition without extra support, assume there is not an individual child who needs individualized instruction or support to begin the transition and score the indicator as *Yes*.

TR7. Examples of effectively guiding individual children include when the teacher provides a visual picture of the next activity or center and provides gentle physical touch to guide the child to move with the rest of the class, the teacher gives a child a visual to guide the child to pick a toy to carry as she transitions to the next center, or a similar support strategy. Effective guidance is not being provided if the teacher picks a child up and carries the child to the next destination or the teacher shows a visual representing the next center and a child proceeds to walk to a different center. A child might need guidance and extra support if he or she seems confused and disoriented about what is happening; the child wanders around at the start of an activity; the child has a "meltdown" when transitions occur; the child stands still, looking aimlessly around the room for a prolonged period of time at the start of an activity; the child does not transition to the new activity; or other scenarios that indicate the child is in need of teacher support or guidance during transitions. If all children are appropriately engaged during transitions, assume children are receiving the support that they need and score *Yes*.

TR8. The focus of this indicator is on ensuring that children are not waiting during transitions with nothing to do. Teachers should plan activities or tasks for children to do while they are waiting during transitions. For example, if children line up at the door while they are waiting for their friends to clean up, the teacher could sing a song with the children, play a guessing game, or prompt the children to tell a friend their favorite story. If children spend time waiting during a transition with nothing to do, score *No* for this indicator.

Item 3. Teachers Engage in Supportive Conversations with Children

SC1. An acknowledgment can be any response the teacher makes to children's communicative initiations, whether the response is positive or negative. Acknowledgment can include, but is not limited to, the following: nodding, saying "Shhh," holding up a finger to let children know that they must wait to speak, responding verbally, or answering and expanding on children's communicative initiations.

SC2. To score *Yes*, you should observe an adult referring to most of the children in the classroom by name at some point during the observation. Adults in the classroom should address children by using their names (e.g., "Jonah, I am so glad you are here today," "Skye, I saw you help your friends clean up.")

SC3. Conversations are defined as brief back-and-forth exchanges that involve a statement or question, a response, and a counterresponse. Conversations do not include interactions in which a teacher is solely giving directions and is not waiting for child responses.

SC4. To score *Yes*, the teacher or other staff should join in children's play and engage in brief conversations about their play at least two times during the observation. The teacher should join in play with children, use toys or materials similar to what children are using, *and* talk about what children are doing.

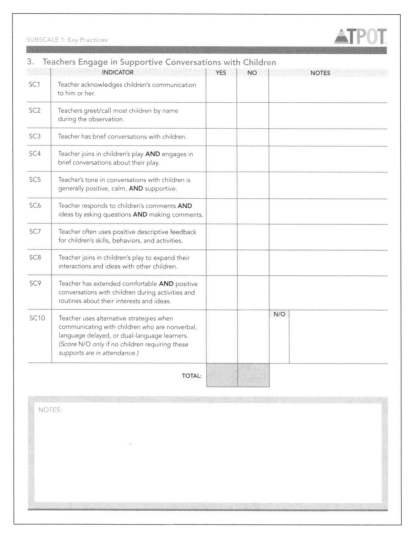

SUBSCALE 1: Key Practices   **ATPOT**

3.   Teachers Engage in Supportive Conversations with Children

	INDICATOR	YES	NO	NOTES
SC1	Teacher acknowledges children's communication to him or her.			
SC2	Teachers greet/call most children by name during the observation.			
SC3	Teacher has brief conversations with children.			
SC4	Teacher joins in children's play **AND** engages in brief conversations about their play.			
SC5	Teacher's tone in conversations with children is generally positive, calm, **AND** supportive.			
SC6	Teacher responds to children's comments **AND** ideas by asking questions **AND** making comments.			
SC7	Teacher often uses positive descriptive feedback for children's skills, behaviors, and activities.			
SC8	Teacher joins in children's play to expand their interactions and ideas with other children.			
SC9	Teacher has extended comfortable **AND** positive conversations with children during activities and routines about their interests and ideas.			
SC10	Teacher uses alternative strategies when communicating with children who are nonverbal, language delayed, or dual-language learners. *(Score N/O only if no children requiring these supports are in attendance.)*		N/O	
	TOTAL:			

NOTES:

Item 3.   Teachers Engage in Supportive Conversations with Children

SC5. Score *No* if the teacher yells at children, uses a harsh voice, is sarcastic with children, or is critical of children.

SC6. To score *Yes* on this indicator, the teacher should frequently respond to children's comments or expressed ideas by asking questions and making comments that acknowledge and then elaborate on children's comments or expressed ideas.

SC7. An example of positive descriptive feedback during play might be, "Wow, you guys were sharing toys and playing together so nicely. The town you built with blocks is so interesting," rather than just, "Nice playing!"

SC8. Beyond joining in play, the teacher helps children expand their interactions with other children, such as by providing suggestions of new themes, new actions, or different ways to interact with materials.

SC9. *Extended* refers to conversations that have multiple turns by both the child and the adult. SC9 differs from SC3 in that conversations are longer and focused explicitly and authentically on children's interests and ideas. For SC3, the adult might have a brief back-and-forth conversational exchange with a child about what the child ate for dinner last night during a pretend-play activity focused on playing restaurant. For SC9, the conversation about what the child had for dinner last night would be longer and would be linked to the child's interests and ideas about dinner that is being served in the pretend-play restaurant.

SC10. Engaging in supportive communication interactions with children with significant disabilities, children with language delays, or dual-language learners often requires a teacher to use different modes of communication and adjust the type and level of language used. Supportive communication interactions with a child with a significant language disability or language delay might look very different than supportive communication interactions with a child who does not have significant disabilities. For children with significant disabilities, communicative exchanges might involve topics that are concrete (focused on getting immediate needs met, requesting items, or commenting on something in the child's immediate environment), simpler language, shorter phrases, and fewer back-and-forth turns. Examples of alternative communication strategies include the use of sign language, conventionalized gestures, speaking in the child's primary or home language, using a picture, speaking in simple sentences, or using the child's assistive or augmentative communication system to interact with the child (e.g., DynaVox, picture symbol exchange). *N/O* should only be scored for this indicator if there are no children in attendance during the observation who are non-verbal, have a language disability or language delay, or who are dual-language learners and would benefit from alternative strategies. Prior to conducting the observation, the observer should ask the teacher the following two questions:

1. "Are there any children present today who are unable to communicate with you in the same way as other children in the class because they have a severe language delay?"

2. "Are there any children present today who need information presented to them in a different way because they are dual-language learners?"

If the teacher replies "No" to both questions, score *N/O*. If the teacher replies "Yes" to either question and the observer did not see any alternative strategies being used with children, score *No*. If the teacher replies "Yes" to either question, *N/O cannot be scored* because the teacher should be communicating with one or more children using alternative strategies during observation.

Item 4. Promoting Children's Engagement

ENG1. Examples of general guidance include the teacher saying, "You could build a tall tower with those blocks," to a group of children who are wandering around the block area but not engaged with the blocks.

ENG2. For this indicator to be scored *Yes*, most activities must be developmentally appropriate and almost all of the class must be engaged in activities that are observed. Long wait times or activities that do not engage almost all children would receive a score of *No* for this indicator. Developmentally appropriate means activities are appropriate for children's ages, interests, experiences, and developmental levels. Children should be engaged (e.g., responding, talking, playing, using materials) in the activities provided.

ENG3. To score a *Yes* on this indicator, teachers must use child-sized chairs or sit on the floor with children during large-group time and activities. Teachers must make an effort to be at the child's level as much as physically possible when having conversations, engaging in play, or interacting with the children across classroom activities. If the teacher is physically unable to sit in small chairs (i.e., due to physical challenges),

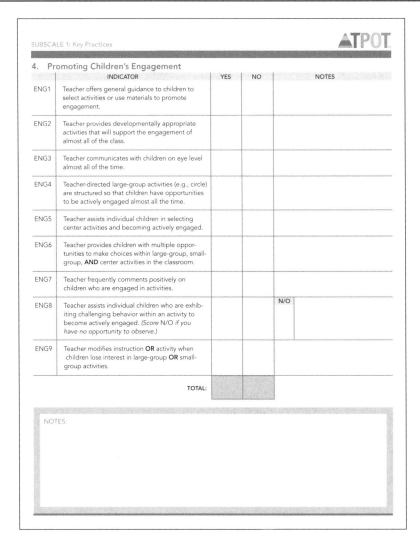

Item 4. Promoting Children's Engagement

then the teacher should make efforts to connect with children at eye level in other ways, such as having children sit in chairs or encouraging children to stand and connect at eye level with the teacher for conversations, if the teacher is seated in a wheelchair.

ENG4. To score *Yes*, large-group activities are designed to offer children multiple opportunities to respond, interact with materials, and make movements. Children do not have to be actively engaged almost all the time to score this as *Yes*, but there must be opportunities where children can be actively engaged almost all the time.

ENG5. To score a *Yes*, the teacher must encourage a child to be actively engaged during centers or other child-directed activities. The child does not have to engage in the activity that the teacher suggests, but the child *must* be actively engaged in some activity in order to score *Yes*. The teacher only has to assist one child in becoming actively engaged for this indicator to be scored *Yes*. An example of a teacher assisting individual children in selecting center activities and becoming actively engaged includes offering materials to promote engagement if a child is not engaged or initiating a new activity in one of the centers, such as getting out Play-Doh or bubbles, to support a child to pick a center and engage in an activity. If all children are engaged throughout all child-directed or center activities during the observation, score this indicator as *Yes*.

ENG6. To score *Yes*, teachers must provide a child or multiple children with opportunities to make choices. This should occur within large-group, small-group (if offered by the teacher), and center activities. To score *Yes*, at least two choices must be offered in each activity that occurs during the observation. The choice opportunity might be offered to one child or to multiple children.

ENG7. To score *Yes*, teacher should comment positively and frequently about children children's appropriate interactions with materials, adults, or peers while an activity is going on. Positive comments focused solely on a product are not considered comments or feedback about engagement. Positive and descriptive comments or feedback about engagement might include adults saying, "Thanks for listening to your friend read the book," "You are working so hard on that picture," or "What a great idea to build the castle using the blocks!"

ENG8. To score *Yes*, the teacher provides assistance to the child who exhibited challenging behavior (exhibiting a challenging behavior is defined as in the Challenging Behavior subscale) to become reengaged within an activity or interaction. The child must become actively engaged for this indicator to be scored as *Yes*.

ENG9. Score *Yes* if a few children (e.g., two or more) lose interest in an activity and the teacher modifies or adjusts the activity to help them reengage. However, if children lose interest in both a large- and small-group activity and the teacher *only* modifies or adjusts in one of them, score a *No*. If children only lose interest in one type of activity (i.e., small-group or large-group) and the teacher modifies instruction or the activity, then score a *Yes*. If all children are engaged in both small- and large-group activities throughout the observation, then you can assume they are getting the support they need and score a *Yes*. If you only observe one type of activity, score this item for the type of activity or activities you observe. For example, if there is a large-group teacher-directed activity and no small-group activity, score *Yes* only if the teacher adjusts the large-group activity. If there are two large-group activities and no small-group activities, score *Yes* only if the teacher adjusts both large-group activities. Please note that adjustments or modifications can be subtle; they might include having children sit near the teacher, providing an extra visual or high-interest item to ensure engagement, or allowing children who have difficulty engaging to respond first.

Item 5. Providing Directions

PD1. To score *Yes*, the majority of directions should be short and specific such that they tell the children what to do without a lot of extra words. Although the length may vary, depending on the age of the children, directions should include the specific actions the teacher expects the children to do. For example, the teacher might say, "Pick your toys up and come to the door" or "Find a partner and sit at the table."

PD2. To score *Yes* on this indicator, the majority of the teacher's directions given during the observation should tell children what to do rather than what not to do. Examples of what *not* to do include, "Do not put that bag in your friend's cubby" and "Stop tapping your friend's shoulder."

PD3. An example of positive descriptive feedback to children who follow the directions is, "You and your friends helped each other clean up the blocks," said to a child who puts the blocks away when the teacher states that it is time to clean up. A nonexample would be saying, "Good job," without stating the behavior for which the child

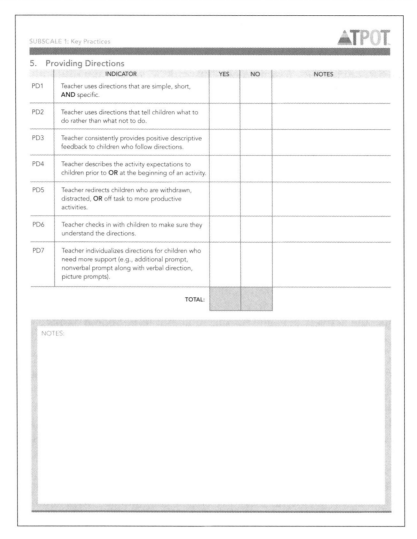

Item 5. Providing Directions

is receiving positive descriptive feedback for following a teacher's direction. The use of positive descriptive feedback should be observed more than a few times during the observation and during at least two different activities to consider it "consistent."

PD4. To score *Yes* on this indicator, the teacher should often provide directions that help children understand the behavior or activity expectations for the activity that is about to begin. For example, before beginning an art activity, the teacher might say, "Be sure you put on your smock before you paint. Then, use your paintbrush to get some paint to make your picture." If the teacher says, "Today we are going to paint butterflies using different colors" this would not be giving children directions to help them understand the behavior or activity expectations for the activity that is about to begin. In another example of providing directions related to activity expectations, the teacher might say, "When we go outside, we have to remember to go down the slide and to walk around the swings."

PD5. This indicator refers to teacher redirection of children who are not following a direction. For example, if children choose the block center at center time but then wander around the room at the start of center time, the teacher might redirect by saying, "You chose the block area today. Why don't you go over to the block center and see what you can find to play?" This indicator is scored as *Yes* if an observer sees a teacher redirect children who are withdrawn, distracted, or off task—regardless of the effectiveness of the redirect. The teacher might miss some opportunities for redirection given the number of children in a classroom, but *Yes* should still be scored if you see the teacher using redirection more often than not when appropriate.

PD6. To score *Yes* on this indicator, the teacher should be observed checking in with individual children or with small groups of children. For example, at clean-up time, the teacher states that children need to put their materials in the appropriate place and then go to the circle area and quietly read a book. When checking in with a small group of children, the teacher might say, "What are you going to do after you clean up your material?" or "What are you going to do once you get to the circle area?"

PD7. For this indicator, if all children are appropriately following directions, then assume that all children are receiving the support that they need and score *Yes*. It does not matter when the teacher provides the individualized directions (e.g., prior to the activity, at the start of the activity). The term *additional prompt* refers to the use of a mode of prompting or supporting children that differs from the form of prompting used with the other children. Examples include breaking a direction into smaller step-by-step components or adding a gesture when repeating the original verbal prompt. If the teacher merely repeats the same verbal prompt given to the larger group or repeats the same prompt over and over to a child who needs more support, score *No*.

Item 6. Collaborative Teaming

CT1. To score *Yes*, adults should be observed to be engaged with children instead of doing paperwork, sitting away from children, or engaging in activities unrelated to what children are doing (e.g., cleaning). If adults are preparing for an activity, talking with parents, observing children and taking notes, or collecting data or assessment information, these activities and routines are considered as being engaged with children.

CT2. To score *Yes*, the tone of conversations between adults should be positive and supportive. Score *No* if you observe adults being harsh with each other at any point during the observation.

CT3. To score *Yes*, the observer should have the sense that the classroom runs like a "well-oiled machine," implying that adults have a plan, know what is next, and know what they need to do. There is not a lot of teacher talk about what they should be doing.

CT4. To score *Yes*, adults (i.e., adults who work in the program or school, not family members) entering the classroom should acknowledge children by speaking to them or engaging in activities with them. Adults should acknowledge or engage briefly with children, even when they enter the classroom for the purpose of speaking with the teacher or taking a child from the classroom. This does not include adults who are quietly entering the classroom to deliver materials, make repairs, or similar custodial activities. However, if children initiate an interaction with adults who are there for custodial or delivery purposes, then adults must respond to the child to score *Yes*. If no adult enters the classroom during the observation, score N/O.

CT5. To score *Yes*, almost all conversations in the classroom between adults who are teachers, program personnel, or other practitioners (i.e., not family members) should be positive, supportive, and related to the children or the classroom activities. Adults should not be discussing personal topics with each other that are not inclusive of

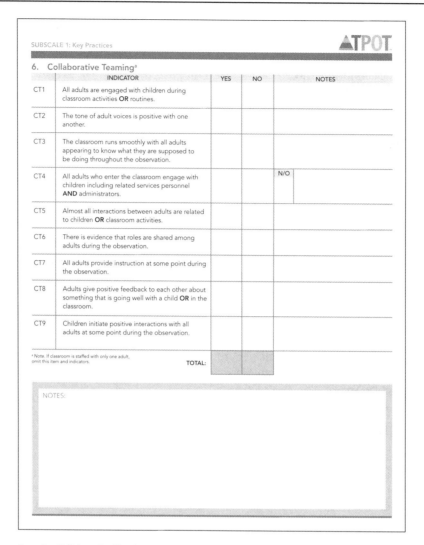

Item 6. Collaborative Teaming

children or do not relate to the classroom (e.g., "Have you seen the new television series on horse racing?").

CT6. To score *Yes*, you should observe teachers and assistants having complementary roles, such as taking turns leading or co-leading activities, working together to clean up or prepare activities, or each talking to families who enter the classrooms. If the assistant is the only one cleaning up and preparing activities during the observation, this indicator would be scored as *No*.

CT7. To score *Yes*, all adults in the classroom are observed either leading a large-group activity, small-group activity, or joining in children's play and having extended interactions/conversations with them during centers. When other professionals enter the classroom, they engage and interact with children as part of the classroom activity. Therapists work with children on their caseloads within the classroom during ongoing activities. If therapists take children out of the classroom but also interact with the child in the classroom in an ongoing activity, score *Yes*.

CT8. To score *Yes*, adults in the classroom provide positive feedback to each other at least two times during the observation. The feedback can be about something that has gone well in the classroom (e.g., "I really like how you arranged the block center activity today") or something positive about an interaction with a child (e.g., "Showing Dawn her visual schedule during the circle to center transition today was a good strategy to help support a smooth transition").

CT9. To score *Yes*, children should be observed initiating positive interactions regularly with all classroom staff during the observation. You should observe multiple children initiating positive interactions with each adult in the classroom during the observation to score *Yes*. It is not necessary for every child to initiate a positive interaction to score *Yes*; however, during the observation, some children must initiate interactions with each adult in the classroom to score *Yes*.

Item 7. Teaching Behavior Expectations

TBE1. Posted behavior expectations or rules should be few in number (i.e., fewer than six expectations, fewer than six rules illustrating a single expectation, fewer than six rules per major activity), include a visual representation (e.g., photograph, drawing), and be

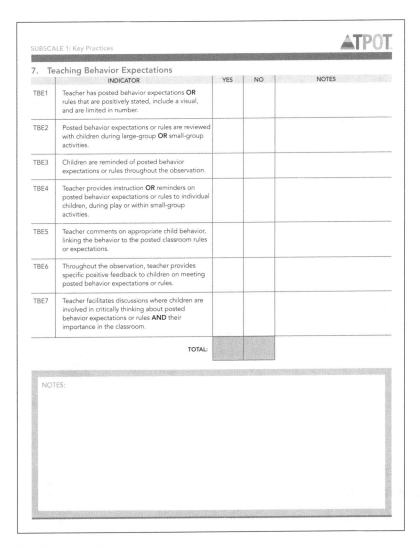

Item 7.   Teaching Behavior Expectations

positively stated (e.g., "Be a team player" and "We use walking feet" rather than "No hitting" and "No running"). In some classrooms, the teacher might post a product from an activity that was conducted with children to identify examples of following rules and expectations. These activity products are not considered when examining criteria for posted rules and expectations. Credit is not given if the posted rule includes both positively stated and negatively stated behavior expectations or rules (e.g., "Use walking feet; do not run"). *Please note that if indicator TBE1 is scored* No, *TBE2–TBE7 must also be scored* No.

TBE2. The teacher reviews posted expectations or rules during large- or small-group activities to score *Yes* on this indicator.

TBE3. Score *Yes* if the teacher provides a whole-group reminder to the class of posted behavior expectations or rules several times during the observation. For example, a teacher might say, "When we go to centers, I want everyone to remember to be a friend and share the toys."

TBE4. Instruction as used in this indicator can be either formal or informal. The teacher can embed instruction on skills related to behavior expectations or rules within ongoing activities. For example, the teacher might set up an opportunity for the children to share a toy and explicitly talk about how the children shared the toy and relate this sharing to a posted class rule or behavior expectation.

TBE5. Score *Yes* if the teacher acknowledges and comments on positive behavior by referring to the expectations or rules (e.g., "You are being a team player" or "You are being safe"). Feedback to the child does not have to include a specific statement about the child's action that links to the rule or expectation to be scored *Yes*. The provision of positive acknowledgment and comments should occur throughout the observation. If the teacher comments on negative behaviors more often than positive behaviors, score *No* even if she comments on positive behaviors.

TBE6. Score *Yes* if the teacher provides positive descriptive and specific feedback to children about their behavior and its relationship to classroom expectations or rules. For example, the teacher might say, "When you helped your friends pick up their toys, you were being a team player." This requires that teachers describe the specific behavior the child is doing and how it relates to the classroom expectation or rule. As with indicator TBE5, this would be scored *No* if the teacher provides feedback that is negative more often than providing feedback that is positive.

TBE7. This indicator is distinguished from TBE4 in that the teacher is helping children think critically about behavior expectations or rules that are posted in the classroom. Building on the sharing example under TBE4, the teacher would expand this interaction by asking questions such as, "What could have happened if you did not share your toy with your friend? How would that make him/her feel? How did you feel when you shared your toy? What are some other times during the day when we can share toys? We read a story about some children who shared. How did it help them share? Why do we share with our friends?" If the teacher only has the children restate the behavior expectations or rules, score *No*. You would also score *No* if the tone of the review is negative, harsh, or placing blame.

Item 8. Teaching Social Skills and Emotional Competencies

In scoring each of these indicators, social skills refers to skills needed for interactions with peers and adults, and emotional competencies refers to skills related to emotion expression, emotion understanding, and emotion regulation.

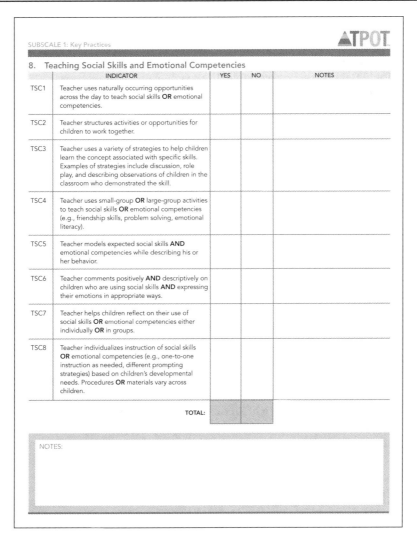

Item 8. Teaching Social Skills and Emotional Competencies

TSC1. To score *Yes* for this indicator, the teacher would routinely use naturally occurring opportunities across the day to teach social skills or emotional competencies. For example, during circle time greeting, the teacher might ask children how they are feeling today. During a small-group activity, the teacher might show one child how to ask a friend for help by showing the child how to tap a friend gently on the arm and telling the child, "Now ask your friend, 'Would you help me?'"

TSC2. To score *Yes*, the teacher should be observed to intentionally structure activities or opportunities for children to work together. For example, a teacher might say, "Choose a friend with whom you want to read a book" or "Find a friend to make friendship pictures with."

TSC3. An example is a teacher describing his or her observations of children in the classroom who demonstrated the skill by saying, "Today I saw children who were playing together and helping each other. During center time, some children were painting a picture together at the art center and some children were helping each other build a tower with the blocks at the block center."

TSC4. This indicator refers to activities that are designed to teach the social *or* emotional skill(s) rather than just talk about the skill(s).

TSC5. To score *Yes* for this indicator, the teacher must model both social skills *and* emotional behaviors. For example, the teacher might model a social skill while describing the behavior by saying, "I am sharing these crayons with my friend," while handing a child some of the crayons. The teacher might model an emotional behavior while describing a behavior by saying, "I am really happy because you are all sitting so nicely on the carpet. I am smiling because I am happy."

TSC6. To score *Yes*, the teacher must comment positively on the behaviors of children who are using appropriate social skills *and* children who express their emotions in positive ways. Examples of positive, descriptive comments are: "Wow, you are really working together to build the house," "Erik, Noah looks so happy because you helped him pick up his toys," "Jace, thanks for asking for a turn with the broom," or "Matilda had a good solution when she got mad. She just walked away."

TSC7. To score *Yes* for this indicator, the teacher must engage a child or children in reflecting on their use of a social skill *or* emotional competency. This discussion should include more child talk than teacher talk. Examples of things the teacher might say are, "What did you do today when your friend was lonely during center time?" or "Tell me what you did today when you wanted the toy Jeff had. Was that a good solution?"

TSC8. A variety of procedures and materials may be used to individualize instruction of social skills *or* emotional competencies, including but not limited to the teacher modeling social skills (e.g. "Look, I am asking my friend for help") for an individual child, role playing scenarios with a child or small group of children, using puppets to model social interactions, using social stories to introduce and review social skills, or using pictures or other visual supports to individualize instruction about expressing emotions.

ITEMS SCORED BY INTERVIEW AND OBSERVATION

It is reasonable to expect that teachers may not explicitly teach all skills associated with indicators for Items 9–11 on the day you are observing. In addition to observing for specific teaching practices related to the indicators for Items 9–11, ask the questions following each item and use your observations and the teacher's answers to the interview questions to score each indicator. Ask the teacher to be as specific as possible throughout the interview. When marking an indicator associated with Items 9–11 as *Yes*, you must also mark *R* (reported), *O* (observed), or both. When scoring an indicator associated with Items 9–11 as *No*, it is not necessary to mark *R* or *O*.

If you observe a behavior that conflicts with teacher report, make scoring decisions based on observation. For example, if the teacher does not describe a practice that you observe the teacher implementing during your observation, give the teacher credit (mark *Yes* and *O* for observed) for the indicator. If the teacher describes the use of a practice (e.g., "I always validate the emotion before I problem solve with a child" or "We always check in using the emotion chart and I always address emotion words during story time") and you do not observe the use of the practices when there are opportunities, mark the indicator as *No* based on your observation. Only mark indicators that counter the teacher's report when you are confident about the decision.

The following rules will help you decide how to score the indicators:

- If you observe the practice associated with the indicator, but the teacher does not report the practice in the interview, mark *Yes* and observed *(O)*.

- If the teacher reports that the practice is used and you see the practice used, mark *Yes* and mark that the practice was reported *(R)* and observed *(O)*.

- If the teacher does not report use of the practice and you do not see the practice used, just mark *No*.

- If the teacher reports the use of a practice and you observe that the teacher did not use the practice as reported, mark *No*.

- If the teacher reports the use of a practice but you observe the use of a practice that is counter to what the teacher reported (e.g., you observe a teacher reprimand a child about expressing emotions, but the teacher reported always validating children's emotions), mark *No*.

- If the teacher reports the use of a practice and there is no opportunity to use the practice during the observation, mark *Yes* and reported *(R)*.

Item 9. Teaching Friendship Skills

Pose the following questions to the teacher:

1. Tell me how you teach or help children to learn how to be friends.

   - What skills do you teach?
   - What strategies and materials do you use?

2. How do you individualize instruction around friendship skills for specific children? Please give me a few examples. (If clarification is requested, you might say, "How do you provide individualized instruction about friendship skills for a child who needs extra help?")

FR1. The teacher suggests that children play together, brings groups of children together and suggests play activities, comments on how to play together, or other actions that communicate to children that playing together is desirable.

FR2. The teacher's comments are positive (e.g., "Wow, look at you!") and descriptive ("I see everyone is being a good friend and taking turns with the train"). Both elements must be in place to be scored *Yes*. Descriptive statements describe specifically what the children are doing.

FR3. This item may be scored as *Yes* if two or more strategies *and* materials are used to teach friendship skills. Strategies might be different ways to teach the same skill. For example, during playtime the teacher might say, "Give Emily the shovel and you take the bucket. You can share." During a story, the teacher might say, "See this picture of two children. One has two trucks and one does not. What can the little girl do to get the other child to play with her?" The term *materials* refers to different objects or instructional materials (e.g., puppets, books, songs).

FR4. Examples of planned opportunities to practice friendship skills include friendship games, role playing, and reading books about friendship skills and then acting them out.

FR5. The teacher shows individual children how to initiate a play interaction (e.g., "If you want to play, you can tap your friend on the shoulder") and respond to a peer (e.g., "He is giving you a car, so he wants you to play cars with him"). Score *Yes* if the teacher indicates that he or she provides (or is observed giving) help to individual children on both forms of social interactions. For example, the teacher might assist one child with

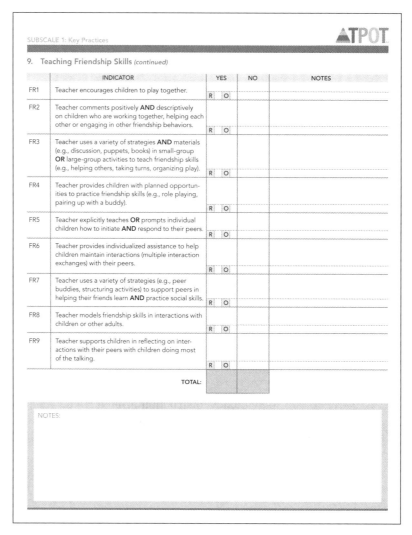

Item 9.   Teaching Friendship Skills

responding to a request to play and help another child with tapping a friend on the shoulder to get the child's attention.

FR6. The teacher assists children to maintain their interactions with peers beyond an initial initiation and response. Maintaining an interaction involves multiple exchanges (i.e., three or more) between children. Assistance might include prompting, giving play suggestions, or helping a child use visual aids or communication devices.

FR7. The teacher is able to identify or the teacher is observed using more than one strategy to support peers to help their friends learn social skills. Examples of strategies include: using peer buddies to support individual children or structuring a play routine for children to make sure that each child has a role and can be actively engaged in social play by taking turns and exchanging materials.

FR8. To model friendship skills, the teacher might descriptively label something he or she does as being a friendship skill. For example, the teacher might say, "I am being a good friend. I am waiting patiently for my turn" or "I am being thoughtful. I let Jo Ellen take the first turn."

FR9. To support children to reflect on interactions with peers, the teacher might report or might be observed posing questions to support children to reflect on interactions with peers. For example, the teacher might say, "Tell me something that someone did to be a friend during centers" or "What happened today when Frances could not get the computer to work?" For children with limited understanding, the teacher might use gestures or sign language (with or without verbal speech) to guide children to reflect on peer interactions.

Item 10. Teaching Children to Express Emotions

Pose the following questions to the teacher:

1. Tell me how you teach or help children recognize and deal with emotions. Give me some examples of the range of emotions you teach or help children learn. (If clarification is requested, you can say, "What are examples of the emotions you help children learn?")

    -   What strategies do you use?
    -   What materials do you use?

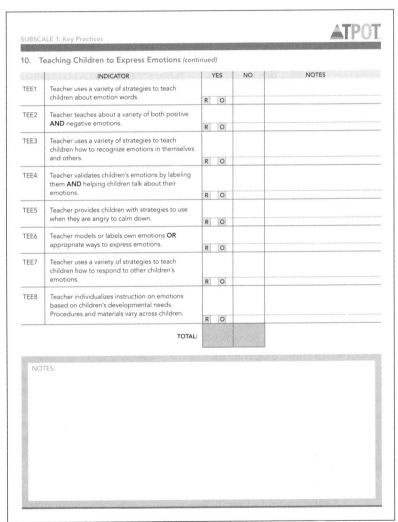

SUBSCALE 1: Key Practices

△TPOT

10. Teaching Children to Express Emotions *(continued)*

	INDICATOR	YES	NO	NOTES
TEE1	Teacher uses a variety of strategies to teach children about emotion words.	R O		
TEE2	Teacher teaches about a variety of both positive **AND** negative emotions.	R O		
TEE3	Teacher uses a variety of strategies to teach children how to recognize emotions in themselves and others.	R O		
TEE4	Teacher validates children's emotions by labeling them **AND** helping children talk about their emotions.	R O		
TEE5	Teacher provides children with strategies to use when they are angry to calm down.	R O		
TEE6	Teacher models or labels own emotions **OR** appropriate ways to express emotions.	R O		
TEE7	Teacher uses a variety of strategies to teach children how to respond to other children's emotions.	R O		
TEE8	Teacher individualizes instruction on emotions based on children's developmental needs. Procedures and materials vary across children.	R O		
	TOTAL:			

NOTES:

Item 10. Teaching Children to Express Emotions

2. Tell me how you teach or help children deal with anger. (If clarification is requested, you can say, "What do you do to help children when they feel angry?")

- What strategies do you use?
- What materials do you use?

3. How do you individualize instruction around emotions for specific children? Please give me a few examples. (If clarification is requested, you can say, "How do you provide individualized instruction about emotions for a child who needs extra help?")

TEE1. To score *Yes*, a variety of strategies or materials are used to teach children emotion words, including talking about them in a large-group activity, reading books with emotion words, commenting on children's emotions using emotion words, playing games with emotion words, or using puppets to talk about emotion words. Score *No* if you only observe one strategy being used.

TEE2. A variety of strategies are used to teach both positive emotions (e.g., happy, proud, excited, glad) and negative emotions (e.g., sad, mad, angry, lonely). Score *No* if only positive or only negative emotions are taught. *No* should also be scored if only one word of each type is taught or discussed.

TEE3. A variety of strategies may be used to teach children how to recognize emotions in themselves and others, including (but not limited to) planned lessons that involve whole-group discussion of different emotions (can be positive and negative emotions), having children identify their own emotions at the start of the day on a classroom chart, reading stories that address emotions, and helping children talk about their emotions and others' emotions (e.g., children, adults) during classroom activities throughout the day.

TEE4. To score *Yes*, the teacher must both label (e.g., "I know you are sad," "I can tell you are excited," "I know you are mad and this is really hard for you") *and* help them talk about their emotions (e.g., "Tell me why you are sad. What made you sad?" "What can you do when you are excited?").

TEE5. To score *Yes*, when children are angry, the teacher prompts children to use strategies such as taking a break, the turtle technique (i.e., a process for calming down when upset), finding something calming to do (e.g., looking at a book, going to the listening center, thinking of something that makes them feel calm, finding a favorite toy, walking away to help calm down).

TEE6. To score *Yes*, the teacher uses emotion language to describe his or her own feelings (e.g., "I am feeling sad today," "It makes me happy when someone offers to help me with my project") or models appropriate ways to respond to emotions (e.g., "When I am mad, I like to go sit by myself until I feel better," "When I am lonely, I like to ask a friend to read a book with me," "When I am scared, I find a teacher").

TEE7. To score *Yes*, the teacher models strategies for children to use to respond to other children's emotions. These strategies include labeling the child's emotions, offering to help a child who is feeling badly, sharing toys with a child who is sad, or asking a friend who is lonely to play.

TEE8. To score *Yes*, the teacher is observed or reports supporting an individual child in ways that are different than the supports provided to a group of children. For example, the teacher might talk about an emotion word during circle time and then walk an individual child through using that word in the context of play when the child is experiencing that emotion. A *Yes* would not be scored for this indicator based on the teacher's actions during the group activity, but a *Yes* can be scored if the teacher supported an individual child to use the emotion word during play. Other ways of individualizing around emotions include reading a book about emotions to an individual child, modeling emotion language for a child, or making an emotions book with a child.

Item 11. Teaching Problem Solving

Pose the following questions to the teacher:

1. Tell me how you teach or help children learn how to solve common social problems in the classroom (e.g., when one child has a toy that another child wants or when a child wants a turn at the computer but another child is there).

    -   What strategies do you use?
    -   What materials do you use?

2. Describe what you teach children to do when they have a social or emotional problem.

3. How do you individualize instruction around problem solving for specific children? Please give me a few examples. (If clarification is requested, you might say "How do you provide individualized instruction about problem solving for a child who needs extra help?")

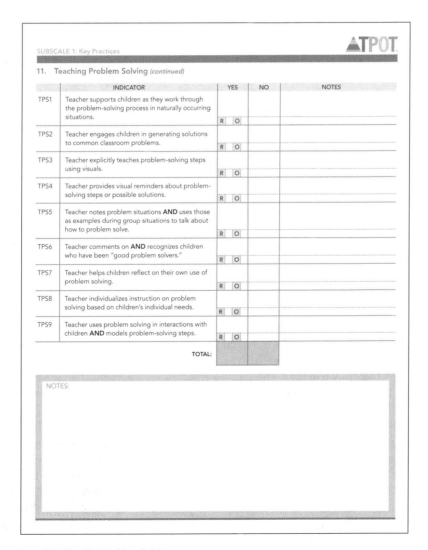

Item 11. Teaching Problem Solving

TPS1. Score *Yes* if the teacher talks to children or demonstrates problem-solving steps during typically occurring activities, including play, group time, transitions, or one-to-one interactions. For example, in response to children who are arguing over a toy, the teacher might say, "If you both want that toy, you could take turns, trade, or do something else. Which one do you want to do?" To score *Yes* for this indicator, all steps of the problem-solving process do not have to be reviewed with the child.

TPS2. The teacher asks children to generate possible solutions to typical classroom problems. For example, the teacher might ask, "We only have one more cracker and two children want a cracker. What could we do?" "It is time to clean up and Adam is not finished with his picture. What could he do?" or "Rya is upset because she wants to play with the computer and two children are already at the computer. What could she do?"

TPS3. To score *Yes*, the teacher must use visuals to teach the use of the problem-solving steps (see definition of problem solving that includes description of steps in Chapter 4). Visuals for problem solving should depict steps that include identifying that the child has a problem and generating a solution.

TPS4. During ongoing activities, the teacher reminds children about the behavior expectations by showing them visuals of the problem-solving steps. This is different than TPS3, which refers to explicit instruction using all the steps of problem solving. To score *Yes* for TPS4, the teacher should remind children of at least some of the steps of the problem-solving process, but the teacher does not have to review all the steps.

TPS5. To score *Yes*, the teacher must be observed or report discussing (during large- or small-group activities) examples of problem situations that have occurred during another time of the day and use those examples to teach children about how to use the problem-solving steps in the future. For example, the teacher might say, "Today I saw children taking toys away from their friends. Next time this happens, what are some things you can do when you want a toy that another child has?"

TPS6. To score *Yes*, the teacher must use positive descriptive feedback to describe a child who has used problem solving. It is not enough for the teacher to quietly provide feedback to the child. The teacher should use it as an example to share with other children about how they can solve problems. For example, the teacher might say, "Today, when Tish wanted a turn on the computer, she told her friend on the computer to come and get her when she was finished" or "When Rahi wanted to use the puzzle Jake had, he asked Jake for the puzzle. When Jake would not give it to him, he found something else to do."

TPS7. To score *Yes*, the teacher must prompt children to talk about how they used problem solving. It is not enough to ask children what they did. The teacher should also ask the children to evaluate a solution in terms of whether it worked and was an appropriate solution.

TPS8. The teacher must provide an explicit example of how he or she individualizes for a child in order to score this as *Yes*. To score a *Yes*, it is not sufficient for teachers to just say that they individualize; they must give an explanation of processes or materials that they use for an individual child that is different than what they do for all other children (e.g., "I have a child who is not able to do this independently, so I have the problem-solving steps on a ring and have to guide him through each step and then physically prompt him to do the selected action.").

TPS9. To score *Yes*, the teacher demonstrates how to solve a problem by saying she has a problem, talking about what she is going to do to solve the problem and then doing it. For example, she might say "I have a problem, I want to play in the water table but there are already four children there. Hmmm, what could I do? I think I will go play in the blocks until someone is finished playing in the water table". Then she goes to the block area and begins playing with children there. The teacher must describe and use at least two of the problem solving steps to score *Yes*.

ITEMS SCORED BY INTERVIEW ONLY

For Items 12–14, ask the teacher to respond to the questions associated with each item. Write down the teacher's responses and use them to score each indicator associated with the item. When scoring these items, the indicator scoring will be based primarily on the teacher's responses to questions. However, you may also use any evidence you observe in the classroom related to the indicator to inform your scoring decisions.

Item 12. Interventions for Children with Persistent Challenging Behavior

Pose the following questions to the teacher:

1. What do you do when children have severe and persistent challenging behavior?

2. What steps do you go through to get support for these children?

3. What is your role in the process of developing a behavior plan for these children?

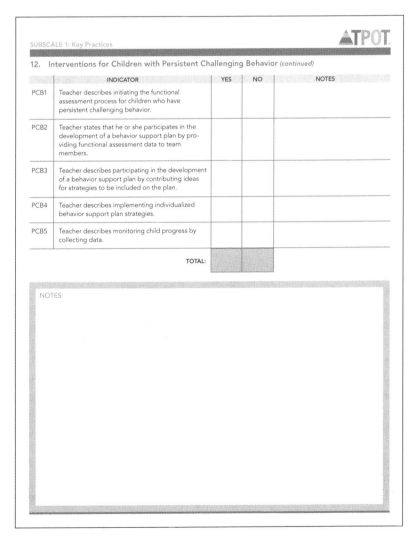

Item 12. Interventions for Children with Persistent Challenging Behavior

4. What is your role in implementing the plan? Tell me how you know if the plan is working.

PCB1. The focus of this indicator is on the initiation of the functional assessment process. Score *Yes* if the teacher reports there is a process for referring the child to a team or individual or describes how he or she begins the functional assessment process (e.g., completing observation cards, collecting data to determine function).

PCB2. The data the teacher collects might include anecdotal records in addition to more formal data used in a functional assessment process (e.g., observation cards, interviews).

PCB3. To score *Yes*, the teacher must report that he or she is part of a team that develops a behavior support plan and that one of his or her roles on the team is to give ideas for strategies that he or she could use in the classroom to address the child's challenging behavior.

PCB4. The teacher must report that he or she implements or follows through with the individualized behavior support plan in the classroom (e.g., "I implement the plan in our activities and routines") but does not have to name explicit strategies or components of the plan.

PCB5. Data collection should include ways to track the outcomes related to the behavior support plan (e.g., behavior incidents, replacement skills, rating scales). If the teacher only mentions using anecdotal records, score *No* for this indicator.

Item 13. Connecting with Families

Pose the following questions to the teacher:

1. Describe how you communicate with your families. What kinds of information do you share with families?

2. Describe how you choose what method you will use to reach families.

3. Describe how you promote family involvement in your classroom.

4. Tell me what you do to make sure *all* families in your classroom can be involved.

COM1. To score *Yes*, the teacher should indicate that there are ways parents can be involved in the classroom on an ongoing basis (e.g., "I have an open door policy," "I strongly encourage all the parents to volunteer or visit our classroom regularly") rather than just on special occasions (e.g., Valentine's Day party).

COM2. To score *Yes*, the teacher must report that the program or the teacher sends home some type of communication to all families multiple times during the year.

COM3. This item is scored based on *classroom observation only*. If there is no evidence of this in the classroom but the teacher mentions having a family book during the interview, the observer can request to view the book to assess the score for this indicator. To score *Yes*, the teacher must show the book to the observer and the book must be available to children in the classroom. If the teacher has to get it out of a cabinet or drawer, this item should be scored as *No*.

COM4. To score *Yes*, the teacher must report that he or she shares information about what is happening in the classroom with parents on a regular basis (at least monthly). If the teacher describes that communication occurs through a general newsletter from the school or program, this indicator should be scored as *No*.

SUBSCALE 1: Key Practices   ▲TPOT.

13.   Connecting with Families *(continued)*

	INDICATOR	YES	NO	NOTES
COM1	Teacher describes, states, **OR** shows documents to indicate that families are offered ongoing opportunities to visit the classroom.			
COM2	Teacher reports that communication to the family comes periodically from the school/program or teacher (e.g., newsletter, open house, parent conferences).			
COM3	Children's families are represented in the classroom (e.g., photographs, family book, bulletin board).[b]			
COM4	Teacher reports that he or she regularly provides families with information on what is occurring in the classroom.			
COM5	Teacher describes a system for regular communication with families that includes celebrations of the child's accomplishments.			
COM6	Teacher describes ways he or she personally connects with families that indicate personal knowledge of the family situation and an appreciation for the family.			
COM7	Teacher states or implies that he or she uses different methods of communication with different families (e.g., home visits, phone calls, classroom visits, notes, newsletter) to ensure that an effort is made to connect with all families.			
COM8	Teacher describes communication systems with families that are bidirectional, offering families a mechanism to share information about the family or child with the teacher.			
	TOTAL:			

[b] This item is scored based on classroom observation only.

NOTES:

Item 13.   Connecting with Families

COM5. To score *Yes*, the teacher must report sending home something (e.g., e-mail, note, log) to each family on a regular basis that addresses how their child is doing and includes information about things the child is doing well. If communication only occurs in this manner at the beginning and end of the year or if the teacher does not specifically indicate that it includes a child's accomplishments, this item should be scored as *No*.

COM6. To score *Yes*, there must be evidence that the teacher communicates with families in a way that indicates he or she knows the unique needs or characteristics of different families. In addition, the communication must include being positive about the family's situation. For example, the teacher might say, "I know it is really hard for Josh's mom to come into the classroom because she works two jobs. However, I sometimes ask her to help make materials for the classroom because I know she really likes to do that and she can do it on her own time." If the teacher says something negative about an individual family, this indicator should be scored as *No* even if it reflects personal knowledge of the family. For example, you would score *No* if the teacher said, "I know it is really hard for Josh's mom to come into the classroom because she works two jobs. She does not seem to want to be involved in the classroom and does not usually follow through when I send things home, so I just keep her updated about what we are doing." This item is different than COM7, which focuses on the mode of communication.

COM7. To score *Yes*, the teacher should describe methods that are differentiated to match family preference or responsiveness. For example, the teacher might state, "Because some of my families do not read, I make sure to call them and describe the upcoming classroom activities."

COM8. The teacher must describe how bidirectional communication systems are used to receive a *Yes* for the indicator (e.g., "I use home–school notebooks and encourage families to write in them before they return them to me to share what is happening at home").

Item 14. Supporting Family Use of the *Pyramid Model* Practices

Pose the following questions to the teacher:

1. What type of information do you provide to families about supporting their children's social-emotional development at home?

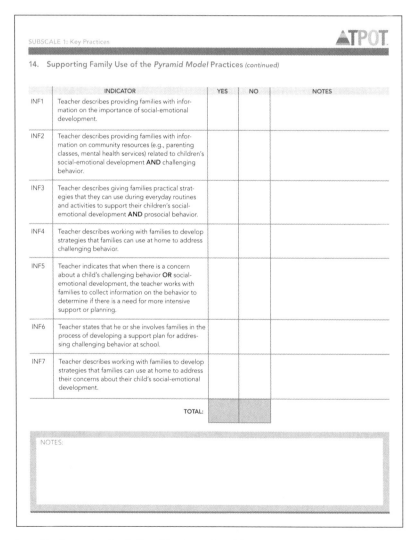

Item 14. Supporting Family Use of the *Pyramid Model* Practices

2. What type of information do you provide to families about addressing challenging behavior at home?

3. Tell me about the role that parents play in supporting their children's social-emotional development at school.

4. Tell me about the role that parents play in addressing children's challenging behavior at school.

INF1. To score *Yes*, the teacher's response should reflect that he or she is intentional in efforts to provide families with information about the importance of social-emotional development. The importance of the information might be implied rather than explicitly stated by the teacher (e.g., "I like to send information about how parents can help their children with sharing and other skills to my families"), but the teacher should describe intentional actions to provide families with information about social-emotional development.

INF2. To score *Yes*, the teacher must report sharing resources related to both social-emotional development (e.g., parent–infant playgroups) *and* challenging behavior (e.g., seminars on addressing challenging behavior at home). Additional examples of community resources include Mother's Day Out or Mommy and Me programs.

INF3. To score *Yes*, the teacher must provide specific examples of materials or information he or she has sent home to families that focuses on promoting social-emotional development and prosocial development (e.g., providing choices to children, friendship skills, communicating emotions). If the teacher only reports sending home information on challenging behavior, score *No* for this item.

INF4. To score *Yes*, the teacher must report that he or she works *with* families to generate strategies for addressing their own child's challenging behavior at home. Score *No* if the teacher only reports sending home suggestions without talking with the family. The focus here is going beyond sending home resources by working with the family to identify strategies that might work for them.

INF5. To score *Yes*, the teacher must provide specific examples of how he or she supports parents to collect information about challenging behavior at home. For example, the teacher might say, "I ask parents to keep a record of five incidences of challenging behavior and what happens before and after them," "I ask families to write down what time of day and during what activity challenging behaviors occur," or "I ask families to complete home observation cards for a few days."

INF6. To score *Yes*, the teacher must report involving families in developing a behavior support plan for use at school. The goal is to have parents provide information and suggestions that could be used at school.

INF7. To score *Yes*, the teacher must provide information on how he or she supports families when they have a concern about their child's social-emotional development (e.g., "The child does not have any friends," "She seems really anxious all the time," "He is so shy, he will not talk to other children").

RED FLAGS

The following are red flags that may represent issues related to teacher training and support or to program policies and procedures. To be scored *Yes*, the red flag should signify a problematic practice in need of immediate attention. Red flags are observable practices that either are counterproductive or not supportive of young children's social-emotional skills or are not appropriate prevention or intervention practices for

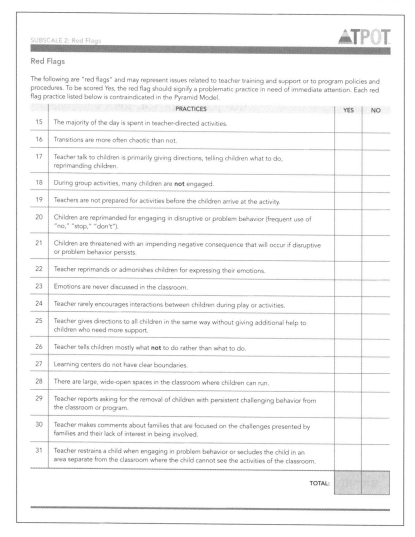

Red Flags

addressing challenging behavior (e.g., teacher reprimands children for expressing their emotions).

15. Score *Yes* if more than 50% of the observation time is spent in teacher-directed activities. See definitions of *teacher-directed* and *child-directed* in chapter 3 of the manual. Base your scoring of this item on the schedule you write down on the score sheet.

16. Score *Yes* if the majority of transitions seem chaotic. If there are only two transitions and one is chaotic, also score *Yes*. In chaotic transitions, children do not seem to know what to do, are wandering, or are not engaged in the transition, or multiple children are having meltdowns.

17. Score *Yes* if this occurs more often than not.

18. Refer to the definition for *engagement* before scoring this item. To score *Yes*, 25% or more of the children should be nonengaged.

19. Score *Yes* if teachers are still gathering materials when children are waiting and ready for an activity. For example, if the children are sitting in circle and the teacher has to get up to get materials for the activity, score *Yes*.

20. Score *Yes* if during the observation children are more often than not reprimanded or admonished for engaging in disruptive or challenging behavior. For this red flag, behavior characterized as disruptive or problematic does not have to meet the definition of challenging behavior in Item 32.

21. Score *Yes* even if you observe only one instance of children being threatened with an impending negative consequence that will occur if challenging behavior persists. This includes the use of threats to move a child to a lower tier on a classroom-wide behavior management system (e.g., "If you do that again, your apple will fall off the tree" or "If you keep doing that, I will have to give you a frowny face.").

22. Score *Yes* even if you observe only one instance of children being admonished or reprimanded for expressing their emotions.

23. Score *Yes* if you observe that the teacher does not describe his or her emotions or children's emotions at any time during the observation. If the teacher mentions emotions only when reprimanding or admonishing children, then you would also score this item as *Yes*.

24. Score *Yes* if the teacher does something to discourage children from working or playing together (e.g., "Do not talk to him while he is trying to paint his picture") or rarely does something specific to encourage children to interact with each other (e.g., "Choose a book and find a friend to look at it with you").

25. If children do not need extra support (e.g., a visual symbol, a sign, repeating the directions to the child directly, reviewing the schedule with the child who needs help), then the teacher may not need to alter the group directions and this red flag can be scored *No*.

26. To score a *Yes* for this red flag, the teacher is observed to often tell children what not to do when providing directions (e.g., "Do not put that bag in your friend's cubby," "Stop tapping your friend's shoulder," "Stop talking and listen to me," "Do not push when you go stand in line"). This red flag is different from Item 21 in that it is related to how teachers in the classroom provide directions.

27. Score *Yes* if learning centers are against walls with no barriers between centers or if it is not possible to determine if there are learning centers.

28. Score *Yes* if there is wide open space that would allow children to run from one side of the classroom to another. This should be an obviously open space.

29. To score a *Yes* for this red flag, the teacher might describe calling a family to pick up a child who has challenging behavior for the day or requesting that the child change classrooms or leave the program. The teacher might comment, "I am hoping that they will find another placement for the child," "There is not much more that we can do for the child. I think another placement is appropriate," "I referred the child to another program," "I told my director that there was nothing more we could do for that child in our classroom," or other statements that indicate that children with challenging behavior should be withdrawn from the classroom.

30. To score a *Yes* for this red flag, the teacher might complain about families; comment that families will not get involved or are not interested in being involved; might comment negatively about families and their lack of interest in their child, the program, or involvement in the program; or might place blame for children's challenging behavior on the family (e.g., "If they would only be consistent with him at home, we would not have these problems at school").

31. Score this item as *Yes* if you see the child being held down by an adult in response to a child's challenging behavior (this does not include blocking a child's response or aggressive action or putting hands on a child); if the child is placed in a chair or device that restricts the child's movement as a response to challenging behavior; or if the child is placed in a time-out area where the child is unable to see other children in the classroom and classroom activities (e.g., time-out room, hall).

Item 32. Using Effective Strategies to Respond to Challenging Behavior

Challenging behavior is defined as behavior that includes 1) physical aggression, such as hitting, kicking, punching, spitting, throwing objects forcefully, pinching, pushing, and biting; 2) climbing on things in the classroom that are not permitted; 3) destroying property, destroying what another child is working on regardless of the other child's response; 4) taking toys away from other children forcefully; 5) running that poses a safety risk for the child or others or elopement from the classroom; 6) tantrum behaviors that might include behaviors such as kicking, screaming, pushing an object or person, stomping feet, or head banging; 7) verbal aggression including yelling, threats, screaming at another person, calling children bad names, and saying bad words; 8) ordering an adult to do something (e.g., "leave me alone"); 9) persistent or prolonged crying that is loud or disruptive or ongoing crying that interferes with the child's engagement in activities; 10) inappropriate use of materials (e.g., jumping off chairs, slamming materials, throwing objects); 11) statements that are noncompliant (e.g., "I'm not going to do it") or clear and explicit verbal or physical refusal to follow directions; or 12) inappropriate touching, stripping, and other behaviors that are hurtful, disruptive, or dangerous to self or others.

This item should be scored in the following manner. First, each incident of challenging behavior is recorded on the scoring form and the essential strategies are scored for each incident recorded. This means that when a child exhibits challenging behavior consistent with the definition, record the incident by briefly describing it (e.g., child cried persistently) and then observe and score the elements based on the strategies the teacher used. Mark *Yes* if the teacher uses the strategy and *No* if the teacher does not use the strategy. Repeat this for each challenging behavior incident that occurs during the observation.

After the observation is complete, you also record if any of the additional strategies were used by the teacher in response to *any* of the behavior incidents. Mark *Yes* for all strategies that you observed the teacher using in response to challenging behavior at any point during the observation. This checklist will be used for coaching teachers, but it will not factor into the score for this item.

The final score for this item is determined as follows:

1. If no incidents of challenging behavior were observed, indicate no incidents observed for the item. No other score is needed.

2. If incidents of challenging behavior occurred and *all* essential strategies were observed in *all* incidents, score *Yes* for the item.

SUBSCALE 3: Responses to Challenging Behavior   △TPOT

32. Using Effective Strategies to Respond to Challenging Behavior *(continued)*

		BEHAVIOR INCIDENT RESPONSE					
	ESSENTIAL STRATEGIES	INCIDENT:		INCIDENT:		INCIDENT:	
		YES	NO	YES	NO	YES	NO
SCB1	Teacher implements developmentally appropriate strategies (e.g., redirection, planned ignoring) in response to challenging behavior.						
SCB2	Teacher responds to children by stating the expected behavior in positive terms (i.e., what to do) or providing instruction in an acceptable alternative behavior.						
SCB3	Teacher provides positive attention or positive descriptive feedback to the child when the child begins behaving appropriately.						
	Summary. Indicate if all three strategies were used:						

Essential Strategies

3. If incidents of challenging behavior occurred but only some of the essential strategies were used in some of the incidents or all three of the essential strategies were used in only some of the incidents, score *No* for the item.

An incident might occur in an activity where the challenging behavior is characterized by its duration (e.g., persistent and prolonged crying) versus an event or single action (e.g., hit, refusal to follow directions). To determine how to identify and segment incidents for coding, note if it is one action versus a duration behavior (e.g., cries off and on throughout circle). Examples of what might be segmented and coded as a single incident of challenging behavior include the following: cries off and on throughout large-group activity (duration in activity); hits child to get toy (single action); or yells "You're stupid" to a teacher (single action). For duration behaviors (e.g., persistent crying), segment the incident by activity. For example, if a child cries off and on throughout circle, record it as one incident and score the indicators based on what the teacher does for the duration of the behavior. If the crying continues during a subsequent transition, record it as a separate incident. If a different challenging behavior occurs by the same child during the activity that the crying is occurring (e.g., hitting an adult), score that as a separate incident.

If a child is taken out of the classroom, do not leave the classroom to continue to observe the strategies used by the staff. If another child has challenging behavior, record the incident and mark any additional strategies that are used by any classroom staff member.

SCB1. The teacher uses strategies that are appropriate for responding to the challenging behavior of young children such as encouraging the child to take a break from an activity, providing a redirection, or ignoring when a child engages in challenging behavior. Score *No* if the teacher is inappropriately harsh, uses physical punishment, or implements a time-out strategy that does not allow the child to return to the activity when ready.

SCB2. To score *Yes* on this indicator, the teacher should respond to the child by stating what the child should do (e.g., "Use your words") or teaching the child what to do (e.g., "Use your words. Tell Emily, 'I want a turn with the truck now'" or "Say, 'Can you move over? You are sitting on my spot.'").

SCB3. To score a *Yes*, the teacher must provide positive attention to the child once challenging behavior ends and the child begins to behave appropriately. Positive attention might include playing with the child, talking to the child, providing the child with

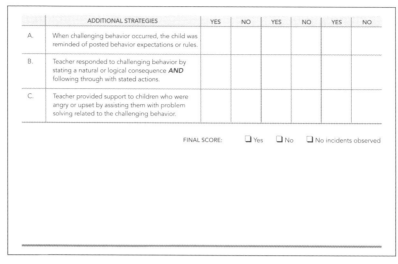

	ADDITIONAL STRATEGIES	YES	NO	YES	NO	YES	NO
A.	When challenging behavior occurred, the child was reminded of posted behavior expectations or rules.						
B.	Teacher responded to challenging behavior by stating a natural or logical consequence **AND** following through with stated actions.						
C.	Teacher provided support to children who were angry or upset by assisting them with problem solving related to the challenging behavior.						

FINAL SCORE: ☐ Yes   ☐ No   ☐ No incidents observed

Additional Strategies

a response opportunity, providing physical affection, or using descriptive comments when the child engages in the appropriate behavior that is the desired alternative to the child's previous display of challenging behavior. Examples of positive descriptive feedback for appropriate behavior include saying, "You are doing a great job sitting with us at circle," or sitting with a child who begins to behave appropriately and saying, "I like how you are sharing the blocks."

SCORING GUIDANCE ON ADDITIONAL STRATEGIES

A. **Reminding child of behavior expectations or rules.** Score this strategy as being used if the teacher reminds the child to use a behavior that is linked to the posted classroom expectations or rules. If there are no posted behavior expectations or rules, then *No* is scored for this indicator.

B. **Logical consequences.** Score this strategy as *Yes* if the teacher states a logical consequence for the intention of redirecting the child to use another behavior *and* follows through with the statement if challenging behavior persists. An example of a logical consequence is, "If you are going to throw the blocks, then we will have to put the blocks away. Keep the blocks on the rug." Putting the blocks away is considered a logical consequence because it is clearly related to the child's inappropriate behavior (the block throwing). You should score *No* for this strategy if the teacher does not state a logical consequence or does not follow through with the consequence. An example of a consequence that is not logical is, "If you are going to throw the blocks, then you will not get to go outside for recess." Keeping the child inside during recess is not a logical consequence because it is not related to the child's inappropriate behavior (the block throwing). To score *Yes* for this strategy, the teacher must pair the logical consequence with a statement of the expected or alternative skill (i.e., tell the child what to do). If the teacher states a logical consequence and challenging behavior is resolved (without the teacher following through with stated action), score a *Yes* for the strategy.

C. **Support problem-solving process.** Score *Yes* for this strategy if the teacher assists the child with the problem-solving process related to the challenging behavior. Problem solving should involve the following or similar steps: identifying the problem (e.g., "Let's think about what your problem was"), identifying potential solutions (e.g., "What can you do when you cannot have a toy?"), evaluating the solutions that are possible, and selecting a solution to try.

CHAPTER 5

Scoring the Teaching Pyramid Observation Tool and Summarizing Results

Chapter 3 described the administration procedures for the TPOT. As noted in Chapter 3, the TPOT scoring form is used during the observation to record notes and responses to interview item questions. In this chapter, we describe how to score the indicators and items on the TPOT and how to summarize the scores.

SCORING INDICATORS FOR KEY PRACTICE ITEMS

The first step in scoring involves reading each indicator associated with each key practice item. To score each indicator, use the notes from the observation and the interview to determine if the practice described in the indicator was or was not observed or was or was not reported to be implemented (for items and indicators that allow teacher report to be used in scoring). The scoring guidance provided for each indicator (see Chapter 4) should be carefully reviewed as scoring determinations are made for each indicator.

Each indicator is scored *Yes* (indicating the practice described in the indicator was observed or reported to be implemented during the interview) or *No* (indicating the practice described in the indicator was not observed or was not reported as being implemented during the interview), unless no opportunity (*N/O*) is listed on the scoring sheet for the indicator. There are four indicators for which N/O is a valid response option: SR8 (The teacher prepares children when changes are going to occur within the posted schedule), SC10 (The teacher uses alternative strategies when communicating with children who are nonverbal, language delayed, or dual-language learners), ENG8 (The teacher assists individual children who are exhibiting challenging behavior within an activity to become actively engaged), and CT4 (All adults who enter the classroom engage with children including related services personnel AND administrators). Every indicator associated with each key practice item should be scored *Yes*, *No*, or *N/O* (when permitted).

Figure 5.1 shows an example of scored indicators associated with the Schedules, Routines, and Activities key practice item. As shown in this figure, practices associated with 8 of the 10 indicators were observed and were scored *Yes* while practices associated with two of the indicators were not observed and were scored *No*. The observer noted that although the teacher did review the posted schedule with children and referred to it throughout the observation, the teacher advised children that centers would not occur that day, given children did not follow a classroom behavior expectation related to listening. Thus, even though the teacher receives credit for preparing children for changes in the schedule (SR8) because she advised children that centers would not occur, she is not given credit for SR3 because this adjustment to the schedule resulted in teacher-directed activities that were longer than 20 minutes.

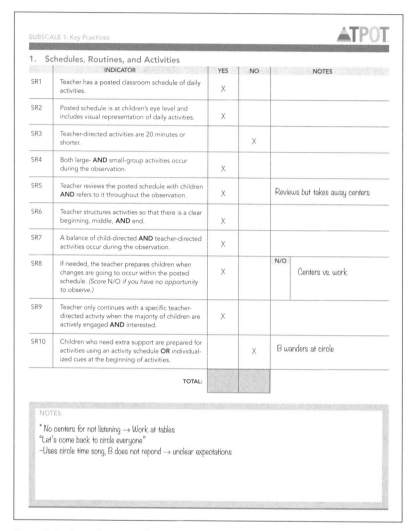

Figure 5.1. Example scoring of indicators associated with Schedules, Routines, and Activities Key Practice item.

Figure 5.2 shows an example of scored indicators associated with the Promoting Children's Engagement key practice item. As shown in this figure, the practices associated with six of the nine indicators were observed and were scored *Yes*, whereas practices associated with three of the indicators were not observed and were scored *No*. The observer noted the teacher provided developmentally appropriate activities that supported the engagement of almost all of the class as described in the scoring guidance for indicator ENG2. However, she did not communicate at eye level almost all of the time as described in the scoring guidance for ENG3. As noted on the scoring form, the teacher was either seated in a chair or standing during circle and during several other activities in which children were engaged. The scoring notes for ENG8 indicate that the teacher did assist an individual child who was exhibiting challenging behavior during an activity to become actively engaged. When the child exhibited persistent crying because the house center was closed, the teacher used responsive strategies to engage the child in an activity in the block center. The observer's notes also list several positive statements made by the teacher when children were engaged in activities to support her *Yes* score for indicator ENG7. The teacher was not observed to provide

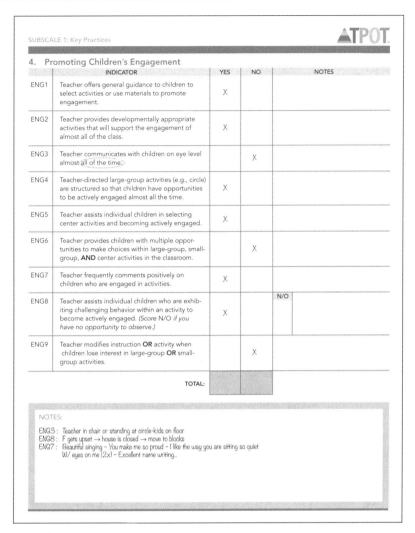

Figure 5.2. Example scoring of indicators associated with Promoting Children's Engagement key practice item.

multiple opportunities for children to make choices within large-group, small-group, and center activities. She also did not modify her instruction or the activity when children lost interest in large-group and small-group activities as defined in the scoring guidance.

SUMMARIZING AND INTERPRETING SCORES ASSOCIATED WITH KEY PRACTICE ITEMS

After indicators associated with each practice item are scored as illustrated in Figures 5.1 and 5.2, summary scores can be obtained for each key practice item. Given that key practice items have different numbers of indicators associated with them, we recommend the summary score be expressed as the percentage of indicators scored *Yes*. This key practice item percentage score is calculated by summing the number of indicators scored *Yes* for a key practice item, dividing by the number of indicators scored either *Yes* or *No*, and multiplying this result by 100. If an indicator is scored *N/O* (which is a scoring option for four indicators: SR8, SC10, ENG8 and CT4), it is not included in the divisor. For the example shown in Figure 5.1, the key practice item percentage score for Schedules, Routines, and Activities is 80% (8 indicators scored *Yes*/10 indicators scored either *Yes* or *No* = 0.8 × 100 = 80%). For the example shown in Figure 5.2, the key practice item percentage score for promoting children's engagement is 67% (6 indicators scored *Yes*/9 indicators scored either *Yes* or *No* = 0.666 = 67%). We recommend rounding to the nearest whole number for ease of interpretation (unless you are using the TPOT for research purposes, for which rounding to one or two decimal places might be appropriate).

Percentage scores for each of the 14 key practice items can be derived. These summary scores might be particularly useful for creating a descriptive profile that summarizes implementation of practices within and across the 14 key practice items or for reviewing progress in practice implementation over time. Figure 5.3 shows a summary profile for an individual teacher. As shown in the profile, this teacher has relative strengths implementing practices related to schedules, routines, and activities; engaging in supportive conversations with children, and collaborative teaming. At the first TPOT administration, her percentage scores for these three key practice items are at or approximately 80%. The teacher's profile suggests the need for implementation support for practices associated with at least seven key practice items (i.e., transitions, providing directions, teaching social skills and emotional competencies, teaching friendship skills, teaching children to express emotions, teaching problem solving, and interventions for supporting children with persistent challenging behavior).

Percentage scores for key practice items can also be compared across successive TPOT administrations. These data are particularly useful for evaluating change in practice implementation over time, perhaps in response to professional development focused on the *Pyramid Model* or in response to other implementation supports. Figure 5.4 shows this teacher's key practice item profile over three successive administrations of the TPOT. At TPOT 1, the teacher had not received professional development on the *Pyramid Model*. At TPOT 2, which was administered 2 months after TPOT 1, she had participated in a 3-day, 19-hour workshop series on the *Pyramid Model* and associated practices. At TPOT 3, administered 5 months after TPOT 2, the teacher had participated in 15 expert coaching sessions in which a practice-based coaching framework (National Center on Quality Teaching and Learning, 2013) was used. As shown in Figure 5.4, this teacher's profile changed over time. By TPOT 3, more indicators associated with the seven key practice items that had TPOT 1 percentage scores of 50% or lower were scored *Yes*. The teacher's percentage scores for each of these key practice items approximated, was equal to, or exceeded 80%.

OBTAINING AND INTERPRETING A KEY PRACTICES SUBSCALE SCORE

To obtain a Key Practices subscale score, the number of indicators scored *Yes* across the 14 key practice items are summed; this number is divided by the number of indicators scored either *Yes* or *No*, and the result is multiplied by 100. If an indicator is scored *N/O* (which is a scoring option for four indicators: SR8, SC10, ENG8, and CT4), it is not included in the divisor. If the collaborative teaming item is omitted because there is only one teacher in the classroom, then the divisor would be reduced by nine (i.e., nine indicators for the teaming item). If every item and indicator is scored *Yes* or *No*, there are 114 indicators on the TPOT. The divisor would be adjusted downward from 114 if *N/O* is scored for any of the four indicators for which *N/O* can be used or if the teaming item is omitted.

A Key Practices subscale score is useful for characterizing overall implementation of *Pyramid Model* practices at a point in time or over time. For the example shown in

Percentage of Indicators Observed for Key Practice Items

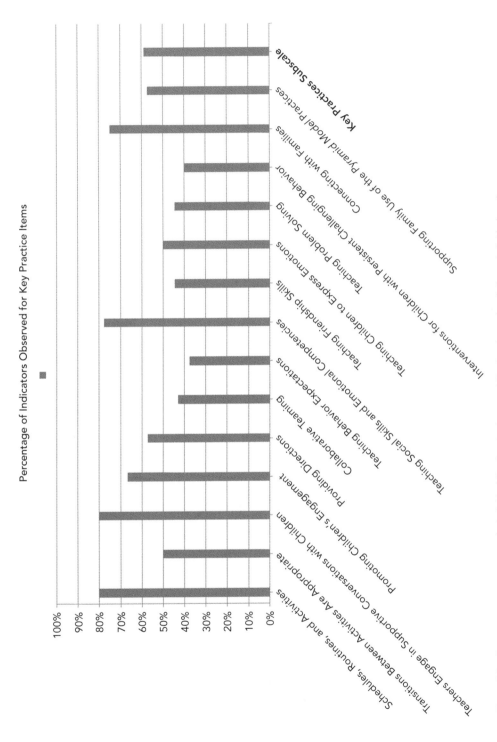

Figure 5.3. Percentage summary scores for individual Key Practice items and Key Practices subscale for an individual teacher.

65

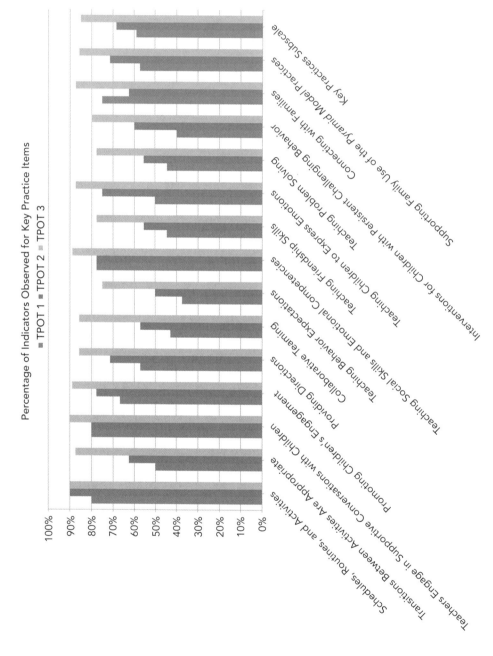

Figure 5.4. Percentage summary scores for individual Key Practice items and Key Practices subscale across three TPOT administrations for an individual teacher.

Figure 5.3, the total number of indicators scored *Yes* across the 14 key practice items was 67 and the total number of indicators scored *Yes* or *No* was 114 (*N/O* was not used). The percentage score for the Key Practices subscale is 59% (67/114 = 0.5877 × 100 = 58.77%). As shown in Figure 5.4, the percentage score for the Key Practices subscale increased for TPOT 2 and TPOT 3 administrations relative to TPOT 1 administration (68% and 85%, respectively for TPOT 2 and TPOT 3).

SCORING RED FLAGS

Each of the 17 red flags is considered an item (Items 15-31) and is scored as *Yes* or *No*. Figure 5.5 shows an example of the scored red flag items for a classroom. As shown in this figure, two red flags were observed in the classroom: Item 16 (transitions are more often chaotic than not) and Item 19 (teachers are not prepared for activities before the children arrive at the activity). The observer saw four transitions during the observation and noted that three of them were chaotic with most children not following the teacher's instructions; there were high levels of child disruptive behavior that resulted in the teacher providing additional directions and guidance to assist children in moving to the next activity. The second red flag, Item 19, was scored as a *Yes* because the observer noted that within three different activities the teacher had to leave the activity area to retrieve materials and children had to wait up to 5 minutes for materials to be arranged before the activity began.

SUMMARIZING SCORES FOR RED FLAGS SUBSCALE

Red flag items are summarized in a Red Flags subscale percentage score. This red flag percentage score is calculated by summing the number of red flags scored *Yes*, dividing by the number of red flags scored either *Yes* or *No*, and multiplying this result by 100. For the example shown in Figure 5.5, the red flag percentage score is 12% (2 red flags scored *Yes*/17 red flags scored either *Yes* or *No* = 0.1176 × 100 = 11.76%). As described in Chapter 2, red flag items indicate practices that should be immediately addressed with teachers because they are counterproductive to the implementation of practices that promote the social and emotional competence of young children.

Figure 5.6 shows a reduction of red flag items as depicted in the Red Flags subscale percentage score. In this example, there were three red flag items scored as *Yes*, resulting in a percentage score of almost 18% (i.e., 17.64%) in the first administration of the TPOT conducted in September. A score of 12% represents two red flag items that were scored as *Yes* in the second administration of the TPOT conducted in January.

SCORING THE RESPONSES TO CHALLENGING BEHAVIOR SUBSCALE

As described in Chapter 3, responses to incidents of challenging behavior are scored in Item 32. This item requires that the observer indicate whether an incident of challenging behavior occurred that met the operational definition of challenging behavior and then identify the response strategies that were used by the teacher by scoring *Yes* or *No* for each essential strategy (SCB1-SCB3) for each incident of challenging behavior. After strategies are scored, the observer indicates if all three essential strategies were used for each incident of challenging behavior by marking *Yes* or *No*. In addition, the observer will note on the score sheet if any additional strategies were used by classroom personnel (strategies A–C) as a response to any of the incidents.

SUBSCALE 2: Red Flags   ▲TPOT

Red Flags

The following are "red flags" and may represent issues related to teacher training and support or to program policies and procedures. To be scored *Yes*, the red flag should signify a problematic practice in need of immediate attention. Each red flag practice listed below is contraindicated in the Pyramid Model.

	PRACTICES	YES	NO
15	The majority of the day is spent in teacher-directed activities.		X
16	Transitions are more often chaotic than not.	X	
17	Teacher talk to children is primarily giving directions, telling children what to do, reprimanding children.		X
18	During group activities, many children are **not** engaged.		X
19	Teachers are not prepared for activities before the children arrive at the activity.	X	
20	Children are reprimanded for engaging in disruptive or problem behavior (frequent use of "no," "stop," "don't").		X
21	Children are threatened with an impending negative consequence that will occur if disruptive or problem behavior persists.		X
22	Teacher reprimands or admonishes children for expressing their emotions.		X
23	Emotions are never discussed in the classroom.		X
24	Teacher rarely encourages interactions between children during play or activities.		X
25	Teacher gives directions to all children in the same way without giving additional help to children who need more support.		X
26	Teacher tells children mostly what **not** to do rather than what to do.		X
27	Learning centers do not have clear boundaries.		X
28	There are large, wide-open spaces in the classroom where children can run.		X
29	Teacher reports asking for the removal of children with persistent challenging behavior from the classroom or program.		X
30	Teacher makes comments about families that are focused on the challenges presented by families and their lack of interest in being involved.		X
31	Teacher restrains a child when engaging in problem behavior or secludes the child in an area separate from the classroom where the child cannot see the activities of the classroom.		X
	TOTAL:		

Figure 5.5. Completed Red Flag items score form page for an individual teacher.

Percentage of Red Flags Observed

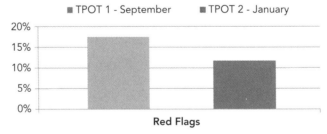

Figure 5.6. Example of red flags scored across two Teaching Pyramid Observation Tool (TPOT™) administrations for an individual teacher.

In Figure 5.7, a completed score sheet for Item 32 is shown. During this observation, two incidents of challenging behavior were recorded as occurring and the observer provided a brief note about what was observed. In one incident, a child threw a box of markers at another child. In the second incident, a child resisted redirection to wash hands by falling to the floor and kicking the classroom teacher.

Figure 5.7. Example of scoring Item 32 for an individual teacher.

In the first incident (throwing the markers), the teacher responded by reminding the child of the classroom expectations ("Joey, throwing the markers is not okay. Throwing can hurt your friends. We need to be safe. If you are angry, you need to use your words.") and asking the child to pick up the markers ("Markers stay on the table. Please pick them up."). After the child picked up the markers and was quietly drawing, the teacher moved to the child and quietly said, "I see that you are working on your drawing and keeping the markers on the table. Tell me about your picture." For the first incident, the observer scored *Yes* for SCB1, SCB2, and SCB3. In addition, the observer noted that the teacher used additional strategy A.

In the second incident, the teacher asked a child to return to the bathroom to wash his hands after toileting. The child responded by shouting "No" and pulling away from the teacher. The teacher blocked the child from leaving the area and restated the request. In response to the second request, the child dropped to the floor and began kicking the teacher. The teacher responded to the behavior by saying, "I am going to wait until you are ready. You must wash your hands before playing. Do not kick me. Kicking hurts." The child continued to kick and shout for a few seconds and then stood up and tried to move past the teacher. The teacher offered, "Why don't I help you wash your hands?" and the

Teacher/Classroom ID: **(enter Teacher/Classroom ID)**

Subscale 1. Key Practices

TPOT Item	TPOT 1 Date: 2/1/2013 # yes	# no	%	TPOT 2 Date: # yes	# no	%	TPOT 3 Date: # yes	# no	%
1 Schedules, routines, and activities	8	2	80%			#DIV/0!			#DIV/0!
2 Transitions between activities			#DIV/0!			#DIV/0!			#DIV/0!
3 Supportive conversations			#DIV/0!			#DIV/0!			#DIV/0!
4 Promoting children's engagement			#DIV/0!			#DIV/0!			#DIV/0!
5 Providing directions			#DIV/0!			#DIV/0!			#DIV/0!
6 Collaborative teaming			#DIV/0!			#DIV/0!			#DIV/0!
7 Teaching children behavior expe...			#DIV/0!			#DIV/0!			#DIV/0!
8 Teaching social skills and emotional competencies			#DIV/0!			#DIV/0!			#DIV/0!
9 Teaching friendship skills			#DIV/0!			#DIV/0!			#DIV/0!
10 Teaching children to express emotions			#DIV/0!			#DIV/0!			#DIV/0!
11 Teaching problem solving			#DIV/0!			#DIV/0!			#DIV/0!
12 Supporting children with persistent challenging behavior			#DIV/0!			#DIV/0!			#DIV/0!
13 Connecting with families			#DIV/0!			#DIV/0!			#DIV/0!
14 Supporting family use of the Pyramid Model Practices			#DIV/0!			#DIV/0!			#DIV/0!
Key Practices Subscale	8	2	80%	0	0	#DIV/0!	0	0	#DIV/0!

ONLY type in GRAY areas

Subscale 2. Red Flags

	# yes	# no	%	# yes	# no	%	# yes	# no	%
15-31 Red flags	1	16	6%			#DIV/0!			#DIV/0!

Subscale 3. Responses to Challenging Behavior

	Yes	No	No Incidents Observed	Yes	No	No Incidents Observed	Yes	No	No Incidents Observed
32 Using Effective Strategies to Respond to Challenging Behavior	0	1	No Incidents Observed	Yes	No	No Incidents Observed	Yes	No	No Incidents Observed
Overall	0%	100%	0%	#####	#####	#DIV/0!	#####	#####	#DIV/0!

1. Enter the teacher or classroom

2. Enter the date of the TPOT.

3. Enter the number of YES and NO responses for each item. If you add the numbers it should equal the number of indicators for that item unless there is an N/O option. If the score is N/O for an indicator, do not count it as a YES or NO response. *If a TPOT is not administered, do not enter any data into the columns. Do not enter

DO NOT TYPE INTO COLUMNS WITH #DIV/0!

DO NOT TYPE IN THIS ROW

4. Enter the number of YES responses for red flags and number of NO

5. Enter a 0 for No and a 1 for YES. If the teacher scored a No for item 32, enter 1 in the No column. In the other 2 columns enter 0.

DO NOT TYPE IN THIS ROW

Figure 5.8. Directions for Microsoft Excel spreadsheet program use.

child responded by moving toward the sink. The teacher washed the child's hands and provided a paper towel to the child to dry his hands. The child left the bathroom and returned to playing. The teacher left the bathroom and began preparing for snack. For this incident, the observer scored SCB1 and SCB2 as *Yes* and SCB3 as *No*.

SUMMARIZING SCORES FOR RESPONSES TO CHALLENGING BEHAVIOR SUBSCALE

The Responses to Challenging Behavior subscale provides a summary related to the use of the three essential strategies in response to challenging behavior. The summary score options are as follows:

Yes: All three essential strategies were used for all incidents of challenging behavior.

No: All three essential strategies were not used for all incidents of challenging behavior.

No incidents of challenging behavior were observed.

In the example presented in Figure 5.7, the teacher was scored *No* because all three essential strategies were not used in response to both behavior incidents.

USING THE SCORING PROGRAM

A Microsoft Excel spreadsheet for scoring the TPOT is available on the Brookes Publishing website at http://www.brookespublishing.com/tpot-scoring-spreadsheet. The Microsoft Excel spreadsheet provides a mechanism to record the scores of a teacher and generate a figure that graphically depicts summary scores. The spreadsheet can be used to record up to three administrations of a TPOT for between 1 and 20 classroom teachers. For each teacher, the spreadsheet provides a graphic summary for each administration and a summary TPOT to show changes in scores over administrations. In addition, the spreadsheet summarizes the scores for multiple teachers in a program by providing an average score across teachers.

To use the spreadsheet, you enter the teacher's name or identification number in the first gray line, as indicated in Figure 5.8. The second step is to enter the date of the TPOT administration in the second line. For each key practice item, count the number of *Yes* and *No* scores and enter into the spreadsheet in the gray box. Use the same procedure to enter the scores for the red flag items. The spreadsheet will automatically calculate the percent scores for each item and for the Key Practices subscale. For Item 32 (Using Effective Strategies to Respond to Challenging Behavior), enter a *1* under the column that indicates your score and a *0* in the other columns. This item has three options for scoring: *Yes* (i.e., all three essential strategies were used for all incidents), *No* (all three essential strategies were not used for all incidents), or *No Incidents* (if no incidents of challenging behavior were observed).

Each tab of the spreadsheet (i.e., Teacher 1, Teacher 2) will accommodate three administrations of the TPOT. The spreadsheet is set up to record the scores of up to 20 teachers. A summary page (final tab of the spreadsheet) will provide the average scores across all teachers entered in the spreadsheet for each TPOT administration.

CHAPTER 6

Using the Teaching Pyramid Observation Tool to Support Implementation of Effective Practices: Case Studies

As described in Chapter 1, the TPOT can be used for a variety of purposes, including as a tool to help inform professional development. Coaching is emerging as an evidence-based professional development practice for supporting teachers' use of teaching and instructional practices such as those included on the TPOT (Fox, Hemmeter, Snyder, Binder, & Clarke, 2011; Hemmeter, Snyder, Fox, & Algina, 2011, Powell & Diamond, 2013; Snyder et al., 2011). Practice-based coaching is one approach to coaching that has promising evidence (National Center on Quality Teaching and Learning, 2013).

A key component of practice-based coaching is the use of needs assessment instruments and associated processes to identify areas of strengths for teachers as well as areas of need related to a specified set of practices. The data from needs assessments can then be used to identify and clarify goals for coaching and to inform the development of action plans. Practices reflected on the TPOT can be used as part of needs assessment processes. TPOT data can be used to identify action plan goals, monitor progress toward action plan goals, and evaluate the effects of coaching on teachers' implementation of *Pyramid Model* practices.

In this chapter, we present two case studies that demonstrate how the TPOT can be used to inform the design, delivery, and evaluation of professional development related to implementation of *Pyramid Model* practices. The first case study illustrates how the TPOT could be used when coaching an individual teacher. The second case study describes the use of the TPOT at the program-wide level to identify professional development needs and then to plan and monitor professional development activities using a data-based decision-making framework.

ELLEN: USING THE TPOT TO PROVIDE IMPLEMENTATION SUPPORT TO A TEACHER THROUGH COACHING-BASED PROFESSIONAL DEVELOPMENT

Ellen is the lead teacher in a state-funded, public preschool classroom. She has been teaching in the public preschool program for 4 years and has a bachelor's degree in child development. Ellen was eager to become an early educator and is motivated to teach because of her love of young children. She finds teaching to be stressful, however. In the past several years, major changes have occurred in the state-funded prekindergarten program, with increased emphasis on early learning standards and the addition of a state-mandated annual child assessment.

Ellen's classroom includes 15 children from 3 to 5 years of age. Of these children, two children are dual-language learners (one speaks Spanish and the other speaks Haitian Creole), and three children have identified disabilities. She has a full-time teaching assistant and the support of a consulting early childhood special education teacher who provides some in-classroom assistance (about 3–5 hours a week) for the children with disabilities. Ellen feels fortunate to have the assistance of her other team members and describes their relationship and ability to work together as strong.

Ellen learned about the *Pyramid Model* through workshops that were offered in her community. She attended a 1-day workshop offered by her school district that provided an overview of the model and associated practices. She was excited about implementing practices to promote social skills and address the behavioral challenges that were occurring in her classroom. After returning to her classroom from the workshops, she was not sure how to begin implementing *Pyramid Model* practices. She quickly became immersed in the daily demands of her classroom and never really got started. The following year, her school district offered additional workshops about the *Pyramid Model* and associated practices as well as implementation support from a coach. A series of 2-hour workshops was offered on early-release days over the course of the school year. Early-release days in her district allowed teachers to have extra planning time or engage in professional development activities.

Ellen recalled her initial excitement about the promise of the *Pyramid Model* and indicated to the district her interest in being part of the professional development. She was intrigued about having the support of a classroom coach, although she was a little worried that coaching sessions might feel uncomfortable or she would not like having someone in her classroom who would be observing and judging her teaching. She attended a district meeting where more information about the workshop series and coaching were described. Her fears about coaching were alleviated when she learned that her coach would not be in an evaluative position and that the coaching process would be driven by her needs and goals related to implementation of *Pyramid Model* practices.

The initial activities that occurred after her enrollment in the *Pyramid Model* professional development were to meet her classroom coach and sign a coaching agreement. The coaching agreement included information on coaching activities and more details about the role of the coach and the teacher in the process. Ellen liked that the coach was enthusiastic about her classroom, listened with empathy when Ellen described many of her challenges with teaching, including dealing with children's behavior challenges, and conveyed a willingness to help Ellen with *Pyramid Model* practice implementation. Once the coaching agreement was signed and Ellen received the schedule of upcoming workshops, Ellen and her coach selected a day for the initial TPOT administration that would occur in her classroom after the first workshop.

The first workshop that Ellen attended included an overview of the *Pyramid Model* and a self-assessment to allow teachers to identify their needs and goals related to *Pyramid Model* practices. The practices included on the self-assessment aligned with many practices included on the TPOT. Ellen indicated on the self-assessment that she needed support to implement practices related to teaching children how to regulate their emotions and to engage in social problem solving. She was eager to implement these practices in her classroom. She was hopeful that if she focused on teaching social and emotional skills with her children, the number of challenging behaviors that were occurring in her classroom would be reduced. Based on her self-assessment of needs, Ellen identified two initial practice goals: 1) learn how to teach children to use the turtle technique for anger management and 2) learn how to teach the problem-solving steps to children.

The coach used the TPOT to guide her first observation in Ellen's classroom the following week. Before beginning the observation, the coach asked Ellen if the children who were dual-language learners and the children with severe language delays were present in the classroom that day. Ellen indicated that they were and discretely indicated who those children were to the coach. Consistent with TPOT administration procedures, the coach spent about 2 hours in the classroom and observed teacher-directed and child-initiated activities as well as transitions between activities. The observation ended when the classroom went outdoors for play. The coach left and returned at the end of the day to conduct the TPOT interview with Ellen. After completing the first observation and interview, the coach scored the TPOT.

In Figure 6.1, Ellen's initial TPOT scores are displayed. Ellen and her coach discussed these TPOT data as the basis for clarifying and verifying Ellen's goals from the needs assessment she completed after the workshop series. Ellen and her coach noted that Ellen's strengths were her implementation of practices related to schedules and routines, supportive conversations, collaborative teaming, interventions for children with persistent challenging behavior, and connecting with families. Overall, she had 47% of all indicators associated with key practice items scored as *Yes.* Two red flags were observed in her classroom, which resulted in a red flag percentage score of 12%, given there were 2 of 17 red flags present (i.e., Item 16, chaotic transitions; Item 20, reprimanding). The red flag score is shown in Figure 6.2.

During the initial TPOT observation, there were five occurrences of challenging behavior, with only one of the essential strategies for responding to challenging behavior being used. The areas noted by Ellen's coach as needing support were practices that would address red flags (i.e., strategies to support effective transitions, teaching children behavior expectations) as well as practices related to teaching social-emotional skills (i.e., friendship skills, emotions, problem solving), and supporting family use of *Pyramid Model* practices.

At the coaching session that occurred the week after the TPOT, the coach and Ellen finalized goals to put on the initial action plan. Ellen discussed the goals she had listed

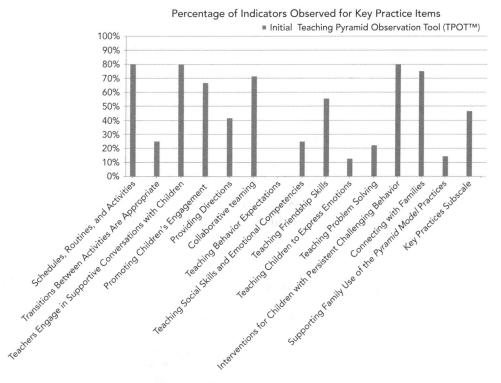

Figure 6.1. Initial key practice item scores for Ellen.

Percentage of Red Flags Observed

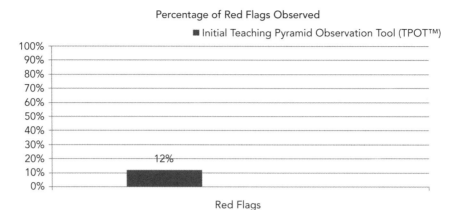

Figure 6.2. Initial Red Flag score for Ellen.

on her needs assessment and the coach and Ellen reviewed data from the TPOT. They discussed areas of strengths and needs. During this discussion, the coach shared her observation that the behavior challenges frustrating Ellen typically were occurring during transitions. The coach described the importance of having carefully planned transitions so children's engagement was supported and children knew what to do during a transition. The coach asked Ellen about her expectations for children's behavior. Ellen responded that she wanted children to be kind to each other, play well together, and take care of materials in the classroom. The coach asked Ellen for ideas about how they could work together to make those expectations clear to the children and to identify opportunities to teach the expectations proactively. Ellen shared that she and her team members usually taught those expectations when redirecting children and that she assumed the children understood what she wanted them to do because it was stated so often each day when children were redirected. The coach described that during the TPOT observation, she saw Ellen and her assistant giving redirections that included statements such as "Be a friend. Ask if you can have a turn," but some children needed more reminders than others and children were only told the expectations when they were already upset and not ready to listen. As they were discussing redirections, Ellen asked for advice about three incidents that occurred during the TPOT observation. She told her coach she was really frustrated with several children who did not respond to redirection. Her coach said she remembered those incidents. She shared that during the observation she noticed Ellen and her assistant were frustrated and their frustration was expressed by reprimanding children (e.g., "Krystal, no running in the classroom") rather than telling children what they should do (e.g., "Krystal, remember to use walking feet in the classroom. Be safe. Use walking feet.").

Following their reflection and discussion, Ellen and her coach developed the initial action plan. They prioritized three goals: 1) establishing and teaching classroom expectations proactively, 2) structuring transitions, and 3) teaching the turtle technique for anger management. The plan included action steps related to each goal, the materials or resources that might be needed, and the timeline for implementing each action step. Action plan goals also included a statement that addressed when each goal would be met and answered the question, "How will I know when I am successful?"

Over the course of the school year, Ellen worked with her coach on the implementation of *Pyramid Model* practices and attended the workshop series. Her coach came to the classroom every 2 weeks and observed Ellen's implementation of practices that were the focus of the action plan during activities, routines, or transitions. Sometimes the coach would model how a practice would be implemented or would bring materials or resources to support Ellen's implementation of practices. The coach and Ellen had a "debrief" meeting after every observation. The debrief meeting always included reflection as well as supportive and constructive feedback about practice implementation. The action plan was used in each debrief meeting and new goals were added to the action plan when appropriate (e.g., goal was achieved, new goal identified). The coach kept what she described as a "running TPOT" each time she observed in Ellen's class. A running TPOT refers to keeping notes on Ellen's progress with practice implementation by looking at TPOT items and indicators and noting what practices were and were not being implemented. The running TPOT provided data that was used to inform the supportive and constructive feedback provided during the debrief meeting.

In late spring, Ellen's coach conducted another TPOT observation and interview. She brought the data (see Figure 6.3 below) to her next coaching session to share with Ellen to demonstrate her progress with the implementation of *Pyramid Model* practices. The TPOT scores showed growth from the initial TPOT administration for all key practice items and no red flags. There was only one incident of challenging behavior, and Ellen used all of the essential strategies in her response. Ellen was very pleased to see her focused effort to implement *Pyramid Model* practices with the support of her coach reflected in her TPOT scores. She reflected that addressing transitions, teaching children behavior expectations, and teaching children social and emotional skills had been pivotal in reducing many of the challenging behaviors in the classroom. She noted that children initiated positive social interactions more often with peers and adults, were helping each other to solve social problems, and were using words or appropriate gestures to express emotions rather than hitting or crying. Ellen asked the coach what she might do to boost her score in teaching friendship skills and supporting family use of *Pyramid Model* practices. The coach identified practices that related to each of these key practice items. She and Ellen discussed which of these practices Ellen wanted to prioritize and together they developed new goals and updated the action plan to reflect these goals.

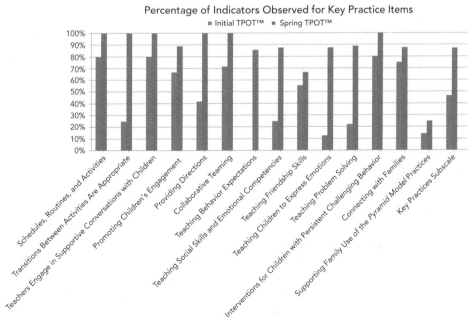

Figure 6.3. Ellen's spring Teaching Pyramid Observation Tool (TPOT™) key practice item scores.

GREEN HILLS CHILD DEVELOPMENT CENTER: USING THE TPOT TO PLAN PROGRAM-WIDE IMPLEMENTATION OF THE *PYRAMID MODEL*

The Green Hills Child Development Center (GHCDC) is a child care program for children 2 to 5 years of age with and without disabilities. They serve 96 children in eight classrooms that are generally grouped by the age of the child. The program contracts with the local education agency to provide services to children with disabilities, including related services such as speech therapy, physical therapy, and occupational therapy. They also enroll children whose families pay tuition and children whose families receive child care subsidies. All lead teachers have at least an associate's degree and several have bachelor's degrees in early childhood education. Each classroom is taught by a lead teacher and an assistant teacher. GHCDC is led by a director and an associate director. The associate director is responsible for family engagement activities and for supporting and coaching teachers.

The GHCDC is accredited by the National Association for the Education of Young Children and the director is committed to providing ongoing professional development to program staff. In the spring of each school year, the director conducts a survey of all teachers to identify professional development needs for the following year. When she received the spring survey data, she noted that the top training need identified by the teachers was related to addressing children's challenging behavior. This identified need was not a surprise to the director and associate director. Over the past year, they had grown increasingly concerned about the number of times they were called to classrooms to help teachers resolve issues related to children's challenging behavior. They also noted that parents were raising concerns about children's challenging behavior at home and in the community. In addition to professional development on the new literacy curriculum they were adopting, they identified a priority need for professional development to improve teachers' competence in addressing challenging behavior.

The director contacted a colleague who worked at a local university to discuss the program's concerns about challenging behavior and asked for suggestions about potential models and professional development strategies for addressing this issue. The colleague mentioned some work that was occurring at the state level around the *Pyramid Model*. The director remembered hearing about the *Pyramid Model* at a meeting but wanted to learn more about it. She was reluctant to begin any new professional development initiative without researching the practices that would be the focus of the professional development (i.e., *Pyramid Model* practices). After learning that there was promising evidence that adopting the *Pyramid Model* and that supporting implementation of *Pyramid Model* practices could address their identified need, she asked her colleague for more information. After receiving information about the *Pyramid Model*, associated practices, and recommendations for supporting practice implementation through professional development, the director shared it with the associate director and the teaching staff. The associate director and many of the teachers were excited about the potential for implementing the *Pyramid Model* program-wide. After reading the materials on the *Pyramid Model* and hearing the associate director and the teachers' enthusiasm about the model, the director called her colleague to determine who could assist the program in implementing the *Pyramid Model*. The colleague connected her to a state technical assistance professional who invited the GHCDC to bring a leadership team to a workshop series on *Pyramid Model* implementation.

The leadership team included the director, associate director, a teacher, a teaching assistant, the speech-language pathologist, and two parents. At the workshop series, the team learned about the critical elements for implementing the *Pyramid Model* program wide and developed a blueprint for implementation. One key component of the blueprint was to develop a professional development plan for supporting teachers in implementation of *Pyramid Model* practices in the classrooms. The team began by planning an overview workshop of the *Pyramid Model* and associated practices for all staff in the program. The goal of this workshop was to introduce all staff to the program-wide *Pyramid Model* that was going to be adopted and to describe what implementation supports would be available. The next step of the blueprint was to identify professional development needs related to program-wide implementation. The associate director attended a TPOT training event and met established interrater agreement criteria. She conducted three TPOT practice administrations with the university colleague who was a certified TPOT trainer and her agreement with the university colleague for each TPOT administration met or exceeded 80% for the Key Practices subscale and Red Flags. She also met agreement standards for the challenging-behavior item. After her training and practice administrations, she administered a TPOT in each classroom. She used a graphing program provided with the TPOT manual to summarize and average key practice item implementation data across teachers. A summary of the TPOT data averaged across the eight GHCDC classrooms is shown in Figure 6.4.

Based on the program-wide TPOT data, the leadership team determined the common areas of need related to implementation of practices associated with each level of the *Pyramid Model*. They decided to focus on the two bottom tiers of the *Pyramid Model*: nurturing and responsive relationships and high-quality supportive environments. They identified three key areas of need that were consistent across most classrooms: 1) difficulty with transitions, 2) nonengagement during large-group activities, and 3) lack of behavior expectations. The program was not able to hold full-day workshops, so the leadership team planned 2-hour workshops on each of these three topics and conducted each workshop twice during naptimes so all teaching teams could attend.

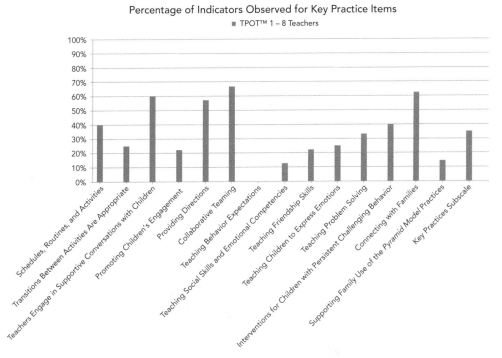

Figure 6.4. Initial Teaching Pyramid Observation Tool (TPOT™) key practice item scores averaged across eight classrooms at Green Hills Child Development Center.

In addition to these common areas of need, the leadership team identified two classrooms and teaching teams (teams 2 and 6) that had additional support needs related to the bottom tiers of the *Pyramid Model*. These teams needed support related to their schedules and the way they provided directions to children. The associate director conducted individual workshops for these teams in addition to the workshops that were being conducted program-wide.

Along with the group trainings, the associate director provided coaching to each teaching team every other week. Coaching was implemented using the processes described above for Ellen. The leadership team decided workshops and coaching would occur during the first 2 months of school, and then they would determine how much progress in practice implementation was being made in the program and in each classroom. In late November, the associate director completed TPOTs in all classrooms. The TPOT data were again summarized and averaged across teachers (see Figure 6.5).

During a December leadership meeting, the team reviewed the TPOT data and determined that, as a whole, the program had made progress on the areas that they had been focused on for the last 2 months. Based on these data, the team determined that they would next focus on the following areas for all teaching teams: 1) teaching friendship skills and emotional literacy and 2) supporting family use of *Pyramid Model* practices. To address these goals, the leadership team provided two additional 2-hour workshops for teachers and a six-session parent group focused on the *Pyramid Model* practices.

The leadership team also analyzed individual teaching team scores. These data indicated the two teams that had received targeted support on specific areas during the preceding few months were doing significantly better in these areas. The associate director continued coaching all teams around the common goals (friendship skills, emotional literacy, supporting family use of *Pyramid Model* practices) and also focused on the areas of need for each teaching team. They also held biweekly teacher meetings to share ideas

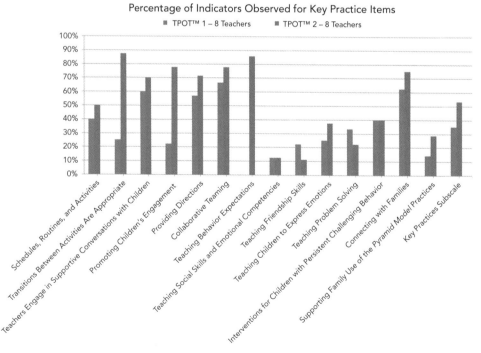

Figure 6.5. November Teaching Pyramid Observation Tool (TPOT™) key practice item scores averaged across eight classrooms at Green Hills Child Development Center.

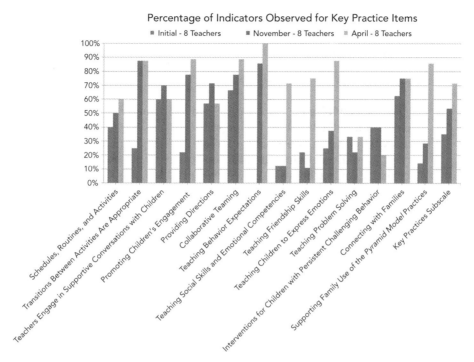

Figure 6.6. April Teaching Pyramid Observation Tool (TPOT™) key practice item scores averaged across eight classrooms at Green Hills Child Development Center.

and engage in problem solving around issues related to *Pyramid Model* implementation. These meetings were voluntary. In April, the associate director once again completed the TPOT in all eight classrooms and summarized the data (see Figure 6.6).

When the leadership team reviewed the April data, they noted the teaching teams made significant progress in the areas that they focused on, particularly around promoting engagement in large-group activities, teaching friendship skills, and supporting family use of *Pyramid Model* practices. Several teams continued to have some difficulty in being systematic about teaching and reinforcing the behavior expectations. They also noted that most of the teams continued to have individual areas where they needed additional support. In addition, they continued to have some children whose behavior was persistent and who needed more individualized support. Although they had supported teachers for these children as needed, they wanted to have a more systematic approach to developing individualized supports. Based on these data, the leadership team developed the following plan for the provision of professional development:

1. The team planned to provide a booster session on teaching and promoting behavior expectations because this was an area of need for most of the teaching teams.

2. The team planned to continue coaching with each teaching team, including identifying two goals that each teaching team wanted to work on during the subsequent 3 months. The leadership team would review the goals identified by each teaching team to determine if there were common areas of need identified for which additional workshops for all teachers could be planned.

3. The team decided to plan a 2-day professional development activity for the week the program would be closed in late summer. During these 2 days, they planned to 1) review the *Pyramid Model* practices they had focused on to date, 2) provide time for teaching teams to reflect on their progress toward implementing *Pyramid Model*

practices, 3) conduct workshops on teaching problem solving and anger management because the TPOT data indicated most teaching teams were not implementing these practices, 4) provide time for teachers to make materials for implementing these practices, and 5) provide time for teachers to discuss ideas for activities and books they could use to teach problem solving and emotional literacy.

4. The leadership team also determined that they wanted to build their capacity to develop individualized behavior support plans for children who needed them. The leadership team made a commitment to hire a consultant to help them design the process, train the associate director to support the process, and provide workshops and coaching for teachers about their role in the process.

CHAPTER 7

Technical Features of the Teaching Pyramid Observation Tool

In this chapter, initial psychometric integrity data for the TPOT are presented. We have organized the presentation of reliability and validity evidence according to the types of inferences or decisions users might want to make about TPOT scores. For example, users might be interested in the extent to which TPOT scores have been demonstrated to be consistent across raters or the extent to which TPOT scores have been shown to relate to scores on other assessment instruments. Users might want to know to what extent indicators associated with each TPOT item are internally consistent. Many users might want information about the extent to which TPOT scores have demonstrated sensitivity to change following a professional development intervention designed to support teachers' fidelity of implementation of *Pyramid Model* practices.

When judging score reliability or validity, rather than implying the TPOT itself is immutably reliable or valid, the type, quality, and extent of available evidence should be judged in relation to proposed uses of scores from the TPOT while considering the characteristics of study samples from whom data were gathered (Crocker & Algina, 2008; Snow & VanHemel, 2008; Thompson, 2003). Therefore, we situate the psychometric integrity evidence available to date by describing characteristics of the study samples with which the TPOT has been used. We provide information about the contexts in which the TPOT was administered and explain how TPOT scores were obtained. We then organize the psychometric evidence under questions likely to be posed by users of the TPOT based on its structure and intended purposes.

Some of the psychometric integrity information presented in this chapter is based on studies conducted using the pilot version of the TPOT (Fox, Hemmeter, & Snyder, 2008; 2009). Other information comes from studies where the research edition of the TPOT has been used. The data from studies that were conducted using the pilot version are reported in this chapter for several reasons. First, as shown in Table 7.1, most items and indicators included on the pilot version were similar in intent and wording to those on the research edition. Second, although indicators included on the pilot version were initially organized under scale anchors of 1, 3, and 5, all data from studies conducted using the pilot version were analyzed at the indicator level using the *Yes*, *No*, and *no opportunity* (when appropriate) scoring categories that are used in the research edition. Third, studies conducted with the pilot version provide initial evidence about the psychometric integrity of TPOT scores pending ongoing studies being conducted with the research edition.

James Algina, EdD co-authored this chapter. We thank him for his important contributions.

Table 7.1. Comparison of pilot version and research edition of Teaching Pyramid Observation Tool

	Pilot version	Research edition
Environmental items (n)	7	0
Learning centers have clear physical boundaries.	Environmental item 1	Red flag 27
The classroom is arranged such that all children in the classroom can move easily around the room.	Environmental item 2	Not included
The classroom is arranged such that there are no large, wide-open spaces where children could run.	Environmental item 3	Red flag 28
There is an adequate number and variety of centers of interest to children and to support the number of children (at least four centers; one center for every four children).	Environmental item 4	Not included
Materials in all centers are adequate to support the number of children allowed to play.	Environmental item 5	Not included
Materials/centers are prepared before children arrive at the center or activity.	Environmental item 6	Red flag 19
Classroom rules or program-wide expectations are posted, illustrated with a picture or photo of each rule or expectation, limited in number (3–5), and stated positively.	Environmental item 7	Teaching Behavior Expectations Indicator 1

	Number of indicators	How indicators scored	Number of indicators	How indicators scored
Key practice items (n = 14)				
Schedules, routines, and activities	9	Observation	10	Observation
Transitions between activities	8	Observation	8	Observation
Supportive conversations	10	Observation	10	Observation
Promoting children's engagement	9	Observation	9	Observation
Providing directions	6	Observation	7	Observation
Collaborative teaming	5	Primarily interview	9	Observation
Teaching behavior expectations	7	Observation	7	Observation
Teaching social skills and emotional competencies	8	Observation	8	Observation
Teaching children to express emotions	8	Observation and interview	8	Observation and interview
Teaching problem solving	10	Observation and interview	9	Observation and interview
Teaching friendship skills	9	Observation and interview	9	Observation and interview
Interventions for children with persistent challenging behavior	4	Primarily interview	5	Primarily interview
Connecting with families	8	Primarily interview	8	Primarily interview
Supporting family use of the *Pyramid Model* practices	7	Primarily interview	7	Primarily interview

	Pilot version	Research edition
Red flag	(n = 16)	(n = 17)
The majority of the day is spent in teacher-directed activities.	✓	✓
Transitions are more often chaotic than not.	✓	✓
Teacher talk to children is primarily giving directions, telling children what to do, reprimanding children.	✓	✓
During group activities, many children are *not* engaged.	✓	✓
Teachers are not prepared for activities before the children arrive at the activity.	✓	✓
Children are reprimanded for engaging in disruptive problem behavior (use of "no," "stop," "don't").	✓	✓
Children are threatened with an impending negative consequence that will occur if disruptive problem behavior persists.	✓	✓
Teacher reprimands children for expressing their emotions.	✓	✓
Emotions are never discussed in the classroom.	✓	✓
Teacher rarely encourages interactions between children during play or activities.	✓	✓
Teacher gives directions to all children in the same way without giving additional help to children who need more support.	✓	✓
Teacher tells children mostly what not to do rather than what to do.	✓	✓
Teacher reports asking for the removal of children with persistent challenging behavior from the classroom or program.	✓	✓
Teacher makes comments about families that are focused on the challenges presented by families and their lack of interest in being involved.	✓	✓
Teacher only communicates with families when children have challenging behavior.[a]	✓	
Teacher complains about other team members and notes difficulty in their relationships.[a]	✓	
Learning centers do not have clear boundaries.[b]		✓
There are large, wide-open spaces in the classroom where children can run.[b]		✓
Teacher restrains a child engaging in challenging behavior or secludes the child in an area separate from the classroom where the child cannot see the activities of the classroom.		✓

Strategies used to respond to challenging behavior	(n = 10)	(n = 6)
Teacher implements developmentally appropriate generic strategies (e.g., redirection, planned ignoring) in response to challenging behavior.[c]	✓	✓
Teacher responds to children by stating the expected behavior in positive terms (i.e., what to do) or providing instruction related to an acceptable alternative behavior.[c]		✓
Teacher provides positive attention or positive descriptive feedback to the child when the child begins to behave appropriately.[c]	✓	✓
When challenging behavior occurred, the child was reminded of posted behavior expectations or rules.[d]	✓	✓
Teacher responded to challenging behavior by stating a natural or logical consequence *and* following through with stated actions.[d]	✓	✓
Teacher provided support to children who were angry or upset by assisting them with problem solving related to the challenging behavior.[d]	✓	✓
Teacher directs children toward a desired alternative behavior.	✓	
Teacher ignores behaviors when appropriate (e.g., behaviors that are not harmful to child or others).	✓	
Teacher responds to problem behavior by using it as a chance to teach an acceptable alternative.	✓	
Teacher uses logical and natural consequences to redirect children to use appropriate behavior.	✓	
Teacher frequently comments on children's appropriate behavior.	✓	

[a]Item was rewritten and included as a key practice indicator in the research edition of the Teaching Pyramid Observation Tool (TPOT™).
[b]Item was included on the pilot version of the TPOT as an environmental item and was modified for the research edition to reflect red flag.
[c]Essential strategy for responding to challenging behavior.
[d]Additional strategy that might be used to respond to challenging behavior.

STUDIES CONDUCTED USING THE PILOT VERSION OF THE TPOT

The pilot version of the TPOT (Fox et al., 2008, 2009) was used with two study samples. Each sample and a brief description of the study in which they participated are described.

Study Sample 1

As part of a larger research project (Hemmeter, Snyder, Fox, & Algina, 2011), the purpose of this psychometric study was to examine TPOT scores with respect to item difficulty, internal consistency, interrater reliability, stability across occasions, and relationships with scores from an instrument designed to measure preschool classroom instructional and interactional quality.

Number, Type, and Location of Classrooms

A total of 50 preschool classrooms in middle Tennessee were included in the study. Thirty-seven were Head Start classrooms, four were early childhood special education classrooms, and nine were prekindergarten classrooms for children at risk.

Sampling

Local programs serving preschool-age children were contacted about study participation. If the program administrator agreed, teachers from the program were contacted to obtain written informed consent.

Characteristics of the Study Sample

The mean age of the lead teachers in the 50 classrooms was 37 years (standard deviation [SD]= 11.5). Twenty-nine teachers identified their ethnicity as African American, 18 reported that they were Caucasian, and 1 teacher reported she was Asian (two participants did not provide information about ethnicity). All teachers were employed full time. The majority of teachers (60%) reported having a bachelor's degree. Eighteen percent had a master's degree, 8% had an associate's degree, 8% reported another type of degree (e.g., Child Development Associate credential, educational specialist), and 6% indicated having a high school degree. The mean number of years of preschool teaching experience was 10.4 (SD = 8.3) and the mean number of years in their present classroom position was 6.7 (SD = 7.0). The average number of children in each teacher's classroom with individualized education programs (IEPs) was two (SD = 2). Eighty-six percent of the teachers reported attending training in the past year on promoting social-emotional skills or addressing challenging behavior. None of the teachers received training by the investigators on the *Pyramid Model* or associated practices during the study. Fifty percent of the teachers reported having children with persistent challenging behavior in their classrooms. Of these teachers, the mean number of children in a classroom with persistent challenging behavior was reported to be three (SD = 3).

Timing of TPOT Observation and Interview

Observations were conducted throughout the preschool year. Each teacher was observed on three occasions and each measurement occasion was separated by 2 weeks.

Study Procedures

The pilot version of the TPOT was administered in each of the 50 preschool classrooms on three occasions by two of six trained data collectors. Observations in each classroom lasted at least 2 hours and included an observation of teacher-directed and child-initiated activities as well as a 10- to 15-minute teacher interview conducted on the same day. Scoring of the TPOT occurred immediately after the observation and interview. Before the first observation occasion, two raters were randomly selected from a pool of six trained raters to score a TPOT in each classroom. The same pair of raters observed on each of the three measurement occasions. Trained data collectors administered the Classroom Assessment Scoring System (CLASS; Pianta, LaParo, & Hamre, 2008) in each classroom between the second and third TPOT measurement occasions. Data collectors attended training conducted by certified CLASS trainers and were trained to CLASS interobserver agreement standards. For each observation, data collectors conducted four observation cycles as recommended in the CLASS manual.

Study Sample 2

The pilot version of the TPOT was used in a potential efficacy trial designed to evaluate the impact of the *Pyramid Model* intervention on preschool teachers' use of Teaching Pyramid practices and children's social skills and challenging behavior. The intervention included a 19.5-hour workshop series provided over 3 days, *Pyramid Model* implementation guides, materials to support implementation of *Pyramid Model* practices in classrooms, and an average of 13 (range: 7-17) instructional, in-classroom coaching sessions provided by trained coaches (Hemmeter et al., 2011). The TPOT was used as a dependent measure to examine fidelity of implementation of *Pyramid Model* practices in both experimental and control classrooms.

Number, Type, and Location of Classrooms

Public school preschool classrooms in Tennessee and Florida that enrolled children without and with or at risk for disabilities were included in the study.

Sampling

Preschool lead teachers from two school districts, one in Tennessee and one in Florida, consented to study participation and were randomly assigned at each site to treatment and control conditions (20 control and 20 intervention) across two cohorts. Cohort 1 had 18 teachers and Cohort 2 had 22 teachers.

Characteristics of the Study Sample

All teachers were female. Forty percent of the teachers held a bachelor's degree, 50% had a master's degree, and 10% had a master's degree plus 30 hours. Sixty-five percent of the sample reported having a degree in early childhood education or early childhood special education. Average years of teaching experience were reported to be 12 (range:<1 to 37 years) and time teaching in current classroom was 5 years (range: <1 to 17 years). There were not statistically significant differences between teachers in the two experimental conditions on any of these variables. The study included 484 (252 intervention and 232 control) preschool-age children enrolled in the 40 teachers' classrooms, of which 104 (56 intervention and 48 control) were identified as target children based on scores in the borderline or clinical range on the Caregiver-Teacher Report Form (CTRF) of the Child Behavior Checklist (CBCL; Achenbach & Rescorla, 2000). Seventy-two percent of the target children had IEPs and 28% had a behavior support plan. The mean age of the target children when the study began was 4 years and the mean length of time the teacher had known the target child when the study began was 6.5 months. There were no statistically significant differences between target children in the two experimental conditions on any of these variables.

Timing of TPOT Observation and Interview

The pilot version of the TPOT was administered on four occasions: 1) preintervention, approximately 5–7 weeks after the school year began; 2) late fall of the same school year, after workshops and early coaching sessions occurred; 3) early spring of the same school year, after workshops and most coaching sessions occurred; and 4) postintervention, at the end of the same school year and after all coaching sessions were completed.

Study Administration Procedures

Trained data collectors conducted TPOTs in each classroom on four occasions by observing child-initiated, teacher-directed, and transition activities for 2 hours and interviewing teachers for 10–15 minutes following the observations. Scoring of the TPOT occurred immediately after the observation and interview. In 44.9% of the TPOT data collection sessions, a second data collector independently completed a TPOT to permit examination of interobserver score agreement. The CLASS (Pianta et al., 2008) data collection occurred in all 40 classrooms on the four measurement occasions previously described. Data collectors attended training conducted by certified CLASS trainers and were trained to CLASS interobserver agreement standards. At each administration of the CLASS, raters conducted four observation cycles according to the CLASS protocol. The Social Skills Improvement System (SSIS; Gresham & Elliott, 2008) was completed by teachers for all children in their classrooms on two occasions (preintervention and postintervention).

STUDIES CONDUCTED USING THE RESEARCH EDITION OF THE TPOT

The research edition of the TPOT is being used to evaluate teachers' fidelity of implementation of *Pyramid Model* practices as part of a larger study involving a randomized controlled efficacy evaluation of the *Pyramid Model* intervention (Hemmeter, Fox, Snyder, & Algina, 2012). Use of the TPOT for Preschool Classrooms Research Edition in the efficacy evaluation began in August 2012 in preschool classrooms located in three school districts in two states (Florida and Tennessee) and is scheduled to be completed in 2016. A brief summary is provided below of the study, the characteristics of the study sample to date, as well as the TPOT administration schedule and study procedures.

Study Sample 3

The purpose of the efficacy trial is to evaluate the impact of the *Pyramid Model* intervention on preschool teachers' use of *Pyramid Model* practices and children's social skills, challenging behavior, and pre-academic skills. The multicomponent intervention includes a 3-day workshop series, *Pyramid Model* implementation guides, materials to support implementation of *Pyramid Model* practices in classrooms, and 16 instructional coaching sessions provided by trained coaches.

Number, Type, and Location of Classrooms

A total of 84 preschool classrooms will be part of the efficacy trial across two enrollment cohorts. The first cohort consists of 40 public school early childhood special education classrooms located in three school districts in Tennessee and Florida that enroll children with or at risk for disabilities or children who are typically developing as part of inclusive classrooms.

Sampling

A total of 40 preschool lead teachers from three school districts, one in Tennessee and two in Florida, consented to study participation as part of cohort one and were randomly assigned at each site to treatment and control conditions (20 control and 20 intervention).

Characteristics of the Study Sample

Of the 40 teachers enrolled to date, 98% were female. Sixty percent of the teachers reported holding a bachelor's degree, 35% reported having a master's degree, and 5% reported having a master's degree plus 30 hours. The percent of the sample reporting that they have a degree in early childhood education, early childhood special education, or special education was 72.8%. Mean years of teaching experience were reported to be 11 (range: <1 to 35 years) and time teaching in current classroom was 4 years (range: <1 to 20 years). There were not statistically significant differences between teachers in the two experimental conditions on any of these variables.

Cohort one included 414 (211 intervention and 203 control) preschool-age children enrolled in the 40 teachers' classrooms, of which 115 (60 intervention and 55 control) were identified as target children based on scores in the borderline or clinical range on the CTRF of the CBCL (Achenbach & Rescorla, 2000). Eighty-seven percent of the target children had an IEP and 16% had a behavior support plan. The mean age of the target children when the study began was 4 years and the mean length of time the teacher had known the target child when the study began was 6.5 months. There were not statistically significant differences between target children in the two experimental conditions on any of these variables.

Timing of TPOT Observation and Interview

Similar to Study 2, the TPOT will be administered on four occasions over the course of the preschool year in experimental and control classrooms. To date, the research edition of the TPOT has been administered preintervention, approximately 5–7 weeks after the school year began for the first cohort of 40 teachers.

Study Administration Procedures

Trained data collectors conducted TPOTs in each classroom by observing child-initiated, teacher-directed, and transition activities for 2 hours and interviewing teachers for 10–15 minutes following the observation. Scoring of the TPOT occurred immediately after the observation and interview. In 14 of the 40 preintervention data collection sessions (35%), a second data collector independently completed a TPOT to permit examination of interobserver score agreement. CLASS (Pianta et al., 2008) and the Early Childhood Environment Rating Scale–Revised (ECERS-R; Harms, Clifford, & Cryer, 2005) data collection also occurred preintervention in all 40 classrooms. Data collectors attended training conducted by certified CLASS trainers and were trained to CLASS interobserver agreement standards. At each administration of the CLASS, raters conducted four observation cycles according to the CLASS protocol. ECERS data collectors were trained following guidelines suggested by Harms et al. (2005).

PSYCHOMETRIC EVIDENCE FOR THE TPOT

In the following sections, we present psychometric evidence available to date for the TPOT based on data obtained from the study samples described above using the pilot version and research edition. A comparison between the pilot version and research edition is provided. Descriptive data are then presented followed by reliability and validity evidence. These latter data are organized under questions likely to be posed by users based on the structure and intended purposes for the TPOT.

Comparison of Pilot Version and Research Edition of the TPOT

Each version of the TPOT used with the three study samples included three subscales: 1) Key Practices, 2) Red Flags, and 3) Responses to Challenging Behavior. Table 7.1 shows a side-by-side comparison of how each of these three subscales is represented on the pilot version and research edition of the TPOT. On the pilot version of the TPOT, there were seven items designated as environmental items. As shown in Table 7.1, these items were either reworded and included as red flags (three items), not included on the research edition because pilot version data showed little to no variability on these items across classrooms (three items), or included as an indicator with slight wording adjustments under a key practice item (one item).

Key Practices Subscale

Both the pilot version and research edition have 14 key practice items. The items are 1) schedules, routines, and activities; 2) transitions between activities; 3) supportive conversations; 4) promoting children's engagement; 5) providing directions; 6) collaborative teaming; 7) teaching behavior expectations; 8) teaching social skills and emotional competencies; 9) teaching children to express emotions; 10) teaching problem solving; 11) teaching friendship skills; 12) interventions for children with persistent challenging behavior; 13) connecting with families; and 14) supporting family use of *Pyramid Model* practices.

Each item has associated practice indicators. There were 108 key practice indicators on the pilot version of the TPOT (four indicators could be scored as *no opportunity*) and there are 114 key practice indicators on the research edition (four indicators can be scored as *no opportunity*). As shown in Table 7.1, for the research edition, one indicator was added to each of three items (i.e., schedules, routines, and activities; providing directions; interventions for children with persistent challenging behavior); four indicators were added to the collaborative teaming item, and the method for scoring indicators associated with this item was changed from primarily interview to observation; and one indicator was deleted from one item (i.e., teaching problem solving).

The score for each item and the score for the Key Practices subscale is computed by 1) summing the number of indicators observed or reported to be implemented (i.e., scored *Yes*), 2) dividing by the number of indicators scored either *Yes* or *No*, and 3) multiplying by 100 to produce a percentage of practices implemented score.

Red Flags

The pilot version of the TPOT had 16 red flags and the research edition has 17 red flags. As shown in Table 7.1, 14 of the red flags are the same across the two versions of the TPOT. Each red flag is scored *Yes* or *No*. Summing the number of *Yes* scores yields a Red Flags subscale score. A red flag percentage score can be calculated by summing the number of *Yes* scores and dividing by 17.

Responses to Challenging Behavior

The subscale includes three indicators reflecting essential strategies that teachers should use to respond to each incident of challenging behavior. Each indicator is scored *Yes* or *No*. As shown in Table 7.1, for the pilot version of the TPOT, when one or more incidents of challenging behavior occurred, TPOT administrators scored 10 indicators *Yes* or *No* based on whether the teacher did or did not use the strategy associated with each indicator to respond to *any* observed incident of challenging behavior. On the research edition of the TPOT, when challenging behavior is observed, each incident of challenging behavior is recorded separately. Observers score the three essential indicators shown in Table 7.1 as *Yes* or *No* based on whether the teacher did or did not use the strategy associated with the indicator to respond to *each* incident of challenging behavior. In addition, Table 7.1 shows three additional indicators for strategies that might be used to respond to an observed incident of challenging behavior. The additional indicators are scored as *Yes* or *No* depending on whether or not strategies associated with the indicator were used in response to any observed incidents of challenging behavior.

Descriptive Statistics

What Do TPOT Scores Tell Us About Preschool Classrooms?

To address this question, data from the first measurement occasion in Study 1 ($n = 50$) and preintervention data from Study 2 ($n = 40$) were combined to create a pilot version sample ($n = 90$). Research edition data reported ($n = 40$) are preintervention data from Study 3. All data presented in this section were collected prior to any training or professional development focused on the *Pyramid Model*. The data presented are descriptive and are not intended to be nationally representative.

Table 7.2 shows percentage score means, medians, standard deviations, and ranges for each key practice item and the Key Practices subscale score across the pilot version and research edition. Key practice item data show that mean percentage scores are similar for 11 of the 14 items across the pilot version and research edition of the TPOT (Cohen's $d = {<}0.5$). Exceptions are collaborative teaming ($d = 1.3$), teaching behavior expectations ($d = 0.6$), and teaching social skills and emotional competencies ($d = 0.5$). For these three items, mean percentage scores are higher for the research edition. Mean percentage scores for the Key Practices subscale were similar across the pilot and research editions (i.e., 41% and 48%, respectively).

The data shown in Table 7.2 indicate that, on average, across the pilot version and research editions, key practice items focused on teaching behavior expectations, teaching social skills and emotional competencies, teaching problem solving, and teaching friendship skills had mean percentage scores of 30% or lower. Items focused on supportive conversations and connecting with families had mean percentage scores of 60% or higher on both the pilot version and research edition.

Table 7.3 shows descriptive statistics for the number of red flags observed across the pilot version and research edition of the TPOT. The mean number of red flags was relatively comparable across the pilot version and research edition (i.e., 3.1 and 3.8, respectively). These data indicate that, on average, about 20% of red flag practices were occurring in preschool classrooms that were part of the study samples. Red flags are inconsistent with or impede implementation of *Pyramid Model* practices.

Descriptive statistics for the Challenging Behavior subscale are shown in Table 7.4. Challenging behavior was observed to occur in 57.8% of TPOT observations conducted using the pilot version and in 82.5% of the observations conducted using the research edition. Although the definition for challenging behavior was somewhat different in the pilot version versus the research edition, it is unlikely the sole explanation for the relatively large difference reported. As shown in Table 7.4, the mean number and percentage of the three essential strategies teachers used to respond to challenging behavior were very similar across the pilot version and research edition. The median number and percentage were identical.

Overall, data gathered using the pilot and research edition of the TPOT indicate that, on average, less than 50% of the indicators associated with the 14 key practice items were scored as *Yes*. Indicators associated with key practice items that involved explicit teaching were scored as *Yes* infrequently. More than 60% of the indicators associated with key practice items related to having supportive conversations with children and connecting with families were scored as *Yes*. On average, 20% of the red flags were observed across both the pilot version and research edition. Challenging behavior occurred more frequently in classrooms included in the research edition sample, although the average numbers of essential strategies used by teachers to respond to challenging behavior were very similar across the pilot version and research edition.

Table 7.2.   Descriptive statistics for key practice items and Key Practices subscale score

Item or subscale	Statistic	Pilot version percentage score (n = 90)	Research edition percentage score (n = 40)
Schedules, routines, and activities	Mean	46.5	47.8
	Median	44.4	44.4
	Standard deviation	22.6	20.4
	Range	0–100	20–90
Transitions between activities	Mean	47.1	58.8
	Median	50.0	62.5
	Standard deviation	25.4	24.4
	Range	0–100	13–100
Supportive conversations	Mean	61.2	61.3
	Median	60.0	60.0
	Standard deviation	18.3	18.2
	Range	20–100	30–100
Promoting children's engagement	Mean	58.5	58.4
	Median	55.6	55.6
	Standard deviation	22.5	19.6
	Range	0–100	13–89
Providing directions	Mean	54.4	64.6
	Median	50.0	57.1
	Standard deviation	24.3	19.4
	Range	0–100	29–100
Collaborative teaming	Mean	45.8	76.1
	Median	40.0	77.8
	Standard deviation	27.2	14.4
	Range	0–100	44–100
Teaching behavior expectations	Mean	12.5	26.1
	Median	0.0	14.3
	Standard deviation	20.5	27.6
	Range	0–86	0–100
Teaching social skills and emotional competencies	Mean	12.6	22.2
	Median	0.0	12.5
	Standard deviation	17.9	18.9
	Range	0–88	0–63
Teaching children to express emotions	Mean	41.9	51.6
	Median	37.5	43.8
	Standard deviation	28.2	31.0
	Range	0–100	0–100
Teaching problem solving	Mean	20.0	23.1
	Median	20.0	11.1
	Standard deviation	18.4	23.4
	Range	0–90	0–78
Teaching friendship skills	Mean	26.2	30.1
	Median	22.2	27.8
	Standard deviation	19.1	22.4
	Range	0–89	0–89
Interventions for children with persistent challenging behavior	Mean	41.4	55.5
	Median	37.5	60.0
	Standard deviation	37.9	33.7
	Range	0–100	0–100
Connecting with families	Mean	64.7	65.0
	Median	62.5	62.5
	Standard deviation	19.1	17.0
	Range	13–100	25–100
Supporting family use of Pyramid Model practices	Mean	34.8	33.6
	Median	28.6	28.6
	Standard deviation	25.0	25.0
	Range	0–100	0–100
Key Practices subscale	Mean	40.5	48.3
	Median	38.0	47.4
	Standard deviation	13.7	15.0
	Range	14–81	22–77

Table 7.3. Descriptive statistics for Red Flags across the pilot version and research edition

Statistic	Pilot version (n = 90)		Research edition (n = 40)	
	Number	Percentage	Number	Percentage
Mean	2.9	18.3	3.8	22.2
Median	2.0	12.5	3.0	17.6
Standard deviation	2.5	15.4	3.1	18.5
Range	0–10	0–63	0–11	0–65

Note. The number of red flags on the pilot version and research edition were 16 and 17, respectively.

Table 7.4. Descriptive statistics for Challenging Behavior subscale across the pilot version and research edition

	Pilot version sample (n = 90)		Research edition sample (n = 40)	
	n	Percentage	n	Percentage
TPOT observation in which challenging behavior occurred	52	57.8	33	82.5
Essential strategies used to respond to challenging behavior (n = 3)				
Mean	1.67	55.8	1.60	69.1
Median	2.00	66.7	2.00	100
Standard deviation	0.92	30.8	1.00	38.9
Range	0–3	0–100	0–3	0–100

Note. Data for the three essential strategies that are part of the Challenging Behavior subscale on the research edition were used for comparative purposes.

To What Extent Do the Key Practice Items on the TPOT Relate to Each Other?

Table 7.5 shows correlations among key practice items using the data from the pilot version samples (*n* = 90) and Table 7.6 shows these correlations using data from the research edition sample (*n* = 40). Across both the pilot version and research edition, many interitem correlations were moderate to strong (i.e., 0.32 to 0.81). Interitem correlations between key practice items reflecting general teaching practices ranged from 0.18 to 0.72. Interitem correlations between key practice items focused on targeted teaching practices ranged from 0.13 to 0.81. The interitem correlation between connecting with families and supporting family use of *Pyramid Model* practices was 0.50 for the pilot version and 0.57 the research edition. On the research edition, the item related to interventions for children with persistent challenging behavior correlated significantly (0.41) with the engagement item; on the pilot version, this item correlated with collaborative teaming (0.22) and with problem solving (0.29) but was not correlated to a noteworthy extent with any other key practice item (range: –0.01 to 0.19).

What Is the Relative Difficulty of the Indicators Associated with the Key Practice Items?

TPOT users often are interested in how difficult it is for a classroom to score a *Yes* on an indicator in the absence of training or professional development focused on *Pyramid Model* practices. To estimate the relative difficulty of each indicator associated with key practice items and for red flags, we used data from the pilot version of the TPOT (*n* = 90 classrooms) and for the research edition (*n*= 40 classrooms). To explore the relative difficulty of the indicators associated with the key practice items or red flags, we examined the percentage of classrooms that received a *Yes* score for each indicator associated with each key practice item and a *Yes* score for each red flag. Table 7.7 shows these data.

Table 7.5. Interitem correlations for Key Practices items: Pilot version (*n* = 90)

	SR	TR	SC	ENG	PD	CT	**TBE**	**TSC**	**TEE**	**TPS**	**FR**	PCB	COM	INF
SR	1.00													
TR	.58**	1.00												
SC	.30**	.41**	1.00											
ENG	.66**	.56**	.57**	1.00										
PD	.53**	.51**	.55**	.60**	1.00									
CT	.18	.16	.28**	.23*	.25*	1.00								
TBE	.12	.28**	.11	.13	.16	.28**	1.00							
TSC	.32**	.41**	.48**	.37**	.37**	.26*	.17	1.00						
TEE	.40**	.41**	.38**	.31**	.48**	.34**	.21	.46**	1.00					
TPS	.38**	.33**	.26*	.31**	.30**	.31**	.16	.41**	.59**	1.00				
FR	.24*	.38**	.24*	.24*	.31**	.28**	.13	.60**	.49**	.54**	1.00			
PCB	.15	.01	.18	.17	.08	.22*	.02	.19	.19	.29**	.06	1.00		
COM	.27*	.15	.37**	.33**	.26*	.49**	.14	.37**	.45**	.35**	.31**	.25*	1.00	
INF	.12	.10	.33**	.17	.27**	.45**	.10	.22	.49**	.53**	.22*	.42**	.50**	1.00

Note. Italicized items are general teaching practices and bolded variables are targeted teaching practices. COM = connecting with families; CT = collaborative teaming; ENG = promoting engagement; FR = teaching friendship skills; INF = supporting family use of *Pyramid Model* practices; PCB = interventions for children with persistent challenging behavior; PD = providing directions; SC = supportive conversations; SR = schedules, routines, and activities; TBE = teaching behavior expectations; TEE = teaching children to express emotions; TPS = teaching problem solving; TR = transitions between activities; TSC = teaching social skills and emotional competencies.
*p < .05. **p < .01.

Table 7.6. Interitem correlations for Key Practices items: Research edition (*n* = 40)

	SR	TR	SC	ENG	PD	CT	**TBE**	**TSC**	**TEE**	**TPS**	**FR**	PCB	COM	INF
SR	1.00													
TR	.45**	1.00												
SC	.64**	.52**	1.00											
ENG	.70**	.59**	.72**	1.00										
PD	.48**	.58**	.60**	.60**	1.00									
CT	.30	.40**	.29	.55**	.34*	1.00								
TBE	.54**	.16	.60**	.51**	.22	.26	1.00							
TSC	.78**	.40**	.65**	.59**	.41**	.14	.48**	1.00						
TEE	.49**	.15	.38*	.51**	.28	.26	.25	.51**	1.00					
TPS	.64**	.36*	.47**	.63**	.38*	.21	.39*	.63**	.58**	1.00				
FR	.59**	.35*	.49**	.57**	.30	.04	.29	.70**	.45**	.81**	1.00			
PCB	.15	.28	.27	.41**	.22	.16	.27	-.04	.11	.08	-.02	1.00		
COM	.63**	.20	.55**	.35*	.37*	.03	.43**	.53**	.29	.47**	.44**	.12	1.00	
INF	.63**	.18	.64**	.52**	.44**	.10	.54**	.62**	.53**	.58	.59**	.20	.57**	1.00

Note. Italicized items are general teaching practices and bolded variables are targeted teaching practices. COM = connecting with families; CT = collaborative teaming; ENG = promoting engagement; FR = teaching friendship skills; INF = supporting family use of *Pyramid Model* practices; PCB = interventions for children with persistent challenging behavior; PD = providing directions; SC = supportive conversations; SR = schedules, routines, and activities; TBE = teaching behavior expectations; TEE = teaching children to express emotions; TPS = teaching problem solving; TR = transitions between activities; TSC = teaching social skills and emotional competencies.
*p < .05, **p < .01.

For each key practice item, there was variability across indicators associated with the item in the percentage of classrooms that received a score of *Yes*. This variability within items is a desirable finding given the structure and purpose of the TPOT. That is, we would expect a larger percentage of teachers to be implementing "easier" indicators associated with a key practice item (e.g., all or almost all teachers will use basic strategies to promote children's engagement) but fewer teachers to be implementing more difficult indicators (e.g., fewer or almost no teachers are individualizing practices to promote a child's engagement). In addition, there are key practice items in which each indicator is less often scored as *Yes*. These are the key practice items that require explicit teaching (e.g., teaching children behavior expectations, teaching children problem solving).

Table 7.7.   Percentage of indicators scored *Yes* for each key practice item and red flags

Key practice item	Indicator	Classrooms scoring *Yes* (%)	
		Pilot version (*n* = 90)	Research edition (*n* = 40)
Schedules, routines, and activities	SR1	54	90
	SR2		63[b]
	SR3	47	13
	SR4	60	80
	SR5	19	18
	SR6	68	58
	SR7	60	33
	SR8	11	17
	SR9	58	53
	SR10	33	40
Transitions between activities	TR1	87	90
	TR2	41	48
	TR3	54	60
	TR4	72	73
	TR5	31	35
	TR6	40	60
	TR7	19	50
	TR8	32	55
Supportive conversations	SC1	100	100
	SC2	100	100
	SC3	87	93
	SC4	64	60
	SC5	91	98
	SC6	60	38
	SC7	32	45
	SC8	20	20
	SC9	27	8
	SC10	29	53
Promoting engagement	ENG1	89	90
	ENG2	84	85
	ENG3	49	58
	ENG4	73	95
	ENG5	52	63
	ENG6	77	10
	ENG7	33	43
	ENG8	30	47
	ENG9	32	35
Providing directions	PD1	94	100
	PD2	84	93
	PD3	22	38
	PD4		55[b]
	PD5	63	80
	PD6	29	40
	PD7	33	48
Collaborative teaming[a]	CT1		100
	CT2		98
	CT3		80
	CT4		65
	CT5		98
	CT6		75
	CT7		80
	CT8		10
	CT9		80
Teaching behavior expectations	TBE1	16	68
	TBE2	27	23
	TBE3	15	20
	TBE4	11	25
	TBE5	11	33
	TBE6	7	13
	TBE7	1	3

(continued)

Table 7.7.   *(continued)*

Key practice item	Indicator	Classrooms scoring *Yes* (%)	
		Pilot version (*n* = 90)	Research edition (*n* = 40)
Teaching social skills and emotional competencies	TSC1	33	80
	TSC2	21	28
	TSC3	6	15
	TSC4	14	20
	TSC5	10	8
	TSC6	11	13
	TSC7	3	3
	TSC8	2	13
Teaching children to express emotions	TEE1	54	75
	TEE2	67	75
	TEE3	43	45
	TEE4	49	45
	TEE5	41	75
	TEE6	42	40
	TEE7	12	23
	TEE8	27	35
Teaching problem-solving	TPS1	62	65
	TPS2	39	25
	TPS3	20	18
	TPS4	2	15
	TPS5	13	15
	TPS6	6	10
	TPS7	8	10
	TPS8	23	35
	TPS9	11	15
	TPS#	16[c]	
Teaching friendship skills	FR1	67	65
	FR2	22	38
	FR3	40	50
	FR4	33	35
	FR5	19	33
	FR6	10	15
	FR7	12	15
	FR8	19	20
	FR9	13	0
Interventions for children with persistent challenging behavior	PCB1	50	65
	PCB2	37	43
	PCB3	49	48
	PCB4	30	68
	PCB5		55[b]
Connecting with families	COM1	79	78
	COM2	98	100
	COM3	20	23
	COM4	92	100
	COM5	41	48
	COM6	31	38
	COM7	89	75
	COM8	68	60
Supporting family use of *Pyramid Model* practices	INF1	27	48
	INF2	30	25
	INF3	33	43
	INF4	33	40
	INF5	47	23
	INF6	64	33
	INF7	9	25
Red flags	RF1	27	63
	RF2	22	15
	RF3	19	35
	RF4	14	18
	RF5	10	0
	RF6	22	15
	RF7	17	31

Key practice item	Indicator	Classrooms scoring *Yes* (%)	
		Pilot version (*n* = 90)	Research edition (*n* = 40)
	RF8	4	8
	RF9	53	28
	RF10	27	48
	RF11	44	25
	RF12	13	10
	RF13		13[d]
	RF14		10[d]
	RF15	6	20
	RF16	10	18
	RF17		25[d]
	RF#	0[e]	
	RF##	3[e]	

Note. Abbreviations for indicators included in the table are those used in the research edition.

[a]Item difficulty values for collaborative teaming indicators were not comparable across pilot version and research edition given changes in method for scoring indicators. Values are reported only for the research edition.

[b]Difficulty for an indicator that was included in the research edition but not the pilot version.

[c]Difficulty for an indicator that was included in the pilot version but not the research edition.

[d]Difficulty for a red flag that was included in the research edition but not the pilot version.

[e]Difficulty for a red flag that was included in the pilot version but not the research edition.

For red flags across both the pilot version and research edition, the proportion of red flags scored as *Yes* ranged from 0% (*Teachers are not prepared for activities before children arrive at the activity*) to 64% (*The majority of the day is spent in teacher-directed activities*). The proportion of red flags was similar across the pilot version and research edition for RF2 (*Transitions are more often chaotic than not;* 22% vs. 15%, respectively), RF4 (*During group activities, many children are not engaged;* 14% vs. 18%, respectively), RF6 (*Children are reprimanded for engaging in disruptive or problem behavior;* 22% vs. 16%, respectively), RF8 (*Teacher reprimands children for expressing their emotions;* 0.04% vs. 0.08%, respectively), and RF12 (*Teacher tells children mostly what not to do rather than what to do;* 13% to 0.10%, respectively).

Score Reliability

Reliability refers to the consistency or stability of scores on an instrument when administration procedures are repeated with a sample of individuals or groups (American Educational Research Association, American Psychological Association, & National Council on Measurement in Education, 1999). Score reliability is reflected in the extent to which random error is minimized. Among the relevant sources of error that could affect TPOT score reliability are raters, occasions of measurement, and items. Each of these is discussed below.

How Are Individuals Trained to Use the TPOT?

One way to reduce random error is to ensure those who are using the TPOT have been trained in its intended use and administration procedures. We have developed and validated TPOT training materials and procedures for use in both our research studies and in TPOT administration workshops conducted at national conferences or in training courses (e.g., National Training Institute, 2013). As part of this training, participants learn about the *Pyramid Model*, practices associated with the model, the intended purposes and uses of the TPOT, administration procedures, and scoring and score interpretation.

During training, participants watch videotaped segments that enable them to score each key practice item, red flags, and challenging behavior. These segments have been coded by at least three TPOT master coders, including the authors of the TPOT, to establish consensus scores. After participants view and score the videotaped segments, trainers discuss participants' scores with them and compare them to the consensus scores. Agreements and disagreements with consensus scores are discussed and scoring guidance for indicators where disagreements with consensus codes are highest is reviewed and used to identify additional training needs. On average, TPOT training takes 6 hours (SD = 1 hour).

After training is completed, users watch one videotape. A classroom observation segment (~2 hours) and an interview segment with a lead teacher (~30 minutes) is part of each videotape, simulating an actual TPOT observation and interview. Training videotapes have been coded by at least three TPOT master coders, including the authors of the TPOT, to establish consensus scores. We recommend users meet or exceed 80% total agreement with consensus codes for at least 1 videotape across all scored indicators for key practice items and red flags. For the challenging behavior item, we recommend users have 80% or greater agreement about the number of incidents of challenging behavior that occur during the observation and 100% agreement about the three essential strategies used for each incident of challenging behavior scored by both observers.

In addition to using videotapes to assess agreement with consensus scores, we recommend users administer the TPOT at least three times in preschool classrooms and evaluate their scores against another trained TPOT observer before administering the TPOT independently. Total score agreement across all scored indicators for key practice items, red flags, and the summary score for responses to challenging behavior should meet or exceed 80% across the three practice administrations.

What Is the Consistency of Scores Across Trained TPOT Observers?

For the three studies in which the pilot version and research edition of the TPOT were used, data collectors were trained using the procedures described above. All met or exceeded the recommended interrater agreement standards before data collection began. In addition, as part of each study, we examined interrater score agreement between pairs of trained raters.

In Study 1, three TPOT observations were conducted in each of 50 classrooms by pairs of trained raters. As noted previously, before the first observation occasion, two raters were randomly selected from a pool of six trained raters to score a TPOT in each classroom. The same pair of raters observed on each of the three measurement occasions. Thus, data were available for 50 rater pairs on three occasions to examine interrater score reliability for each key practice item across each measurement occasion. Generalizability coefficients (Cronbach, Gleser, Nanda, & Rajaratnam, 1972; Shavelson & Webb, 1991) are shown in Table 7.8. Maximum likelihood estimates of the variance components (VC) due to classroom, rater, and error were calculated. Each generalizability coefficient used the VC due to classroom as the numerator and the sum of the VCs as the denominator. This is a conservative generalizability coefficient because it assumes that in routine use of the TPOT, data will be collected using a different rater for each classroom, whereas typically the raters are the same in all or in subsets of classrooms. The results indicate that interrater score reliability and agreement are very

Table 7.8. Generalizability coefficients by occasion for Study 1 using the pilot version in 50 classrooms

Item	Occasion 1	Occasion 2	Occasion 3
Schedules, routines, and activities (*n* = 9)	.68	.65	.68
Transitions between activities (*n* = 8)	.74	.70	.68
Supportive conversations (*n* = 10)	.72	.75	.81
Promoting children's engagement (*n* = 9)	.64	.71	.60
Providing directions (*n* = 6)	.68	.43	.68
Collaborative teaming (*n* = 5)	.51	.60	.63
Teaching behavior expectations (*n* = 7)	.72	.62	.80
Teaching social skills and emotional competencies (*n* = 8)	.78	.78	.73
Teaching children to express emotions (*n* = 8)	.66	.68	.76
Teaching problem solving (*n* = 10)	.56	.71	.74
Teaching friendship skills (*n* = 9)	.74	.74	.62
Interventions for children with persistent challenging behavior (*n* = 4)	.51	.53	.56
Connecting with families (*n* = 8)	.65	.70	.62
Supporting family use of *Pyramid Model* practices (*n* = 7)	.60	.58	.55
Key Practices subscale (*n* = 108)	.89	.93	.90
Red flags (*n* = 16)	.84	.90	.88

Note. Measurement occasions were separated by 2 weeks for each of the 50 teachers.

good to excellent for the Key Practices subscale (≥0.89) and for the Red Flags subscale (≥0.84).

Interrater score reliability coefficients were generally acceptable for key practice items, usually exceeding 0.60 across each of the three measurement occasions. The exception was the item related to interventions for children with persistent challenging behavior, which had coefficients across the three measurement occasions ranging from 0.51 to 0.56.

How Stable Are Scores Across TPOT Administrations?

To examine the stability of TPOT scores, we used data from Study 1, in which three TPOT observations were conducted in each of 50 classrooms by pairs of trained raters. No training or professional development related to the *Pyramid Model* and associated practices was provided during the study to permit examination of score stability across three measurement occasions.

One important aspect of score stability is stability of individual differences (SID), the degree to which teachers' scores on a TPOT variable maintain the same positions relative to one another. SID can be assessed by examining correlation coefficients for scores collected at different occasions. Table 7.9 shows correlations for each TPOT item, as well as the Key Practices and Red Flags subscales. The results indicated that, in general, teachers whose implementation of key practices resulted in relatively high scores on the first measurement occasion also engaged in practices that resulted in relatively high scores on the second and third occasions. Stability coefficients were highest for the key practice item related to schedules, routines, and activities and lowest for collaborative teaming and connecting with families.

Another important aspect of score stability is stability of means over occasions of measurement. Table 7.10 shows that average percentage scores for each key practice item were generally very stable across time. These data show that over the three occasions of measurement when no professional development or training was provided, scores on the TPOT remained stable or showed slight declines. In addition, the average percentage scores for each key practice item across each measurement occasion show that most indicators associated with key practice items were not being scored as *Yes*, with the exception of connecting with families for which, on average, about 60% of the practice

Table 7.9.   Correlation coefficients by item and occasion pair for Study 1 using the pilot version with 50 teachers

Item or subscale	Occasions		
	1 and 2	2 and 3	1 and 3
Schedules, routines, and activities	.85	.74	.75
Transitions between activities	.51	.56	.46
Supportive conversations	.72	.79	.66
Promoting children's engagement	.63	.71	.53
Providing directions	.61	.60	.59
Collaborative teaming	.55	.49	.37
Teaching behavior expectations	.66	.48	.59
Teaching social skills and emotional competencies	.74	.67	.72
Teaching children to express emotions	.73	.65	.58
Teaching problem solving	.66	.78	.55
Teaching friendship skills	.64	.76	.66
Interventions for children with persistent challenging behavior	.59	.66	.51
Connecting with families	.47	.50	.41
Supporting family use of *Pyramid Model* practices	.43	.66	.42
Key Practices subscale	.91	.87	.85
Red flags	.69	.80	.67

Note. Measurement occasions were separated by 2 weeks for each of the 50 teachers.

Table 7.10.   Average percentage scores for key practice items across three measurement occasions in Study 1 using the pilot version in 50 classrooms

Item	Occasion 1	Occasion 2	Occasion 3
Schedules, routines, and activities	45.9	45.0	41.0
Transitions between activities	49.0	45.0	39.0
Supportive conversations	60.8	55.2	55.2
Promoting children's engagement	55.8	54.0	48.0
Providing directions	51.7	44.0	43.3
Collaborative teaming	50.0	44.4	38.0
Teaching behavior expectations	11.4	9.1	8.0
Teaching social skills and emotional competencies	15.0	14.3	12.8
Teaching children to express emotions	47.3	43.0	41.5
Teaching problem solving	24.0	22.6	18.8
Teaching friendship skills	29.1	26.0	23.8
Interventions for children with persistent challenging behavior	39.0	45.0	39.5
Connecting with families	67.0	61.8	61.3
Supporting family use of *Pyramid Model* practices	39.7	37.1	39.7
Key Practices subscale	41.9	38.9	36.4
Red flags	16.4	20.1	19.9

Note. Measurement occasions were separated by 2 weeks for each of the 50 teachers.

indicators were scored as *Yes* on each occasion. Thus, implementation of practices associated with the *Pyramid Model* as measured by scores of *Yes* on TPOT indicators was stable across time but remained at low levels across the three measurement occasions.

What Is the Relationship of Each Key Practice Item to the Key Practices Subscale?

Table 7.11 shows correlations between scores on each key practice item and the Key Practices subscale. With the exception of the key practice item related to interventions for children with persistent challenging behavior on both the pilot version and research edition, collaborative teaming on the research edition, and teaching behavior expectations on the pilot version, item scores tend to be substantially correlated with scores on the Key Practices subscale. This means the Key Practices subscale score represents a good overall summary of practice implementation.

Table 7.11. Item-to-total correlations: Key practice items with Key Practices subscale

Key practice item	Pilot version (n = 90)	Research edition (n = 40)
Schedules, routines, and activities	.65	.85
Transitions between activities	.65	.58
Supportive conversations	.65	.82
Promoting children's engagement	.68	.87
Providing directions	.68	.63
Collaborative teaming	.53	.41
Teaching behavior expectations	.34	.63
Teaching social skills and emotional competencies	.66	.79
Teaching children to express emotions	.75	.64
Teaching problem solving	.69	.79
Teaching friendship skills	.60	.72
Interventions for children with persistent challenging behavior	.36	.33
Connecting with families	.60	.62
Supporting family use of *Pyramid Model* practices	.57	.76

What Is the Internal Consistency Score Reliability for Each Key Practice Item and for the Key Practices and the Red Flag Subscales?

To examine internal consistency score reliability, we used data from the pilot version samples ($n = 90$) and from the research edition sample ($n = 40$). Table 7.12 shows the internal consistency score reliability estimates for each key practice item and for the Key Practices and Red Flag subscales. These estimates are reported as coefficient alpha, which is a single-administration estimate of the reliability of the scores reported on a single occasion. Alpha values typically range from 0.0 to 1.00, although negative values are possible. Higher internal consistency score reliability is desirable. Coefficient alpha can be influenced by several factors, including the number of indicators associated with an item or subscale, the variances of the indicators, and the correlations among the indicators. Typically, alpha increases as each of the three factors increase. In addition, the variance of an item or subscale tends to increase as each of the three factors increase. These dynamics are important to consider when interpreting the coefficient alpha values reported in Table 7.12, particularly for items where the number of indicators or the range of scores for an item is small.

Table 7.12. Coefficient alpha for each key practice item, Key Practices subscale, and Red Flags

Key practice item	Pilot version (n = 90)	Research edition (n = 40)
Schedules, routines, and activities	.58	.58
Transitions between activities	.68	.74
Supportive conversations	.63	.67
Promoting children's engagement	.63	.54
Providing directions	.62	.39
Collaborative teaming	.47	.41
Teaching behavior expectations	.75	.82
Teaching social skills and emotional competencies	.69	.65
Teaching children to express emotions	.74	.82
Teaching problem solving	.68	.77
Teaching friendship skills	.56	.68
Interventions for children with persistent challenging behavior	.78	.72
Connecting with families	.55	.35
Supporting family use of *Pyramid Model* practices	.62	.58
Key Practices subscale	.92	.94
Red flags	.70	.71

For the pilot version of the TPOT, the lowest alpha was 0.47 for the five-indicator collaborative teaming item. The median alpha value was 0.66. Alpha for the 114-indicator Key Practices subscale was 0.92. Coefficient alpha for the Red Flags subscale was 0.70. For the research version of the TPOT, the lowest alpha was 0.35 for the 8-indicator item measuring connecting with families. The median alpha value was 0.67. Alpha for the 114-indicator Key Practices subscale was 0.94. Coefficient alpha for the Red Flags subscale was 0.71.

Across both the pilot version and research edition, the internal consistency score reliability estimates for both the Red Flags and the Key Practices subscales are considered good to excellent, providing initial evidence that scores on these two subscales are sufficiently reliable for both research and other intended purposes for the TPOT.

Score Validity

Score validity refers to evidence that supports the adequacy and appropriateness of inferences made or actions taken from scores derived from measurement (Messick, 1993). This means score validity must be considered in relation to each proposed use of an instrument. For example, users of the TPOT might be interested in the extent to which scores are associated with other instruments designed to measure classroom quality or various dimensions of quality, such as emotional support or instructional support. Other users might be interested in whether TPOT scores are sensitive enough to detect change in implementation of *Pyramid Model* practices when teachers participate in professional development.

Perspectives about validity and what constitutes validity evidence have evolved over time. Current conceptualizations focus on sources of validity evidence rather than types of validity (Snyder, McLean, & Bailey, 2013). We consider several sources of evidence for score validity discussed in the *Standards for Educational and Psychological Testing* (American Educational Research Association et al., 1999) and in the National Research Council (2008) report: 1) evidence based on relationships with other variables, 2) evidence of change in scores following a professional development intervention, and 3) evidence of relationships between teachers' implementation of *Pyramid Model* practices and child outcomes.

To What Extent Are TPOT Scores Related to Scores on Other Instruments Designed to Measure Classroom Quality?

Although the TPOT is not intended to be a measure of classroom quality, we have hypothesized that practices represented by select TPOT indicators are more likely to be implemented with fidelity in classrooms that demonstrate global quality as measured by the ECERS-R (Harms et al., 2005) or instructional and interactional quality as measured by CLASS (Pianta et al., 2008). Therefore, we have examined the extent to which scores on each key practice item, the Key Practices subscale, and red flags are related to scores on each ECERS-R subscale as well as the ECERS-R overall score and each CLASS dimension and domain.

To conduct these exploratory analyses with the ECERS-R, we used data from the research edition of the TPOT ($n = 40$ classrooms). Correlation coefficients are shown in Table 7.13. Relationships between overall global classroom quality as measured by the ECERS-R and the Red Flags subscale on the TPOT were generally moderate and negative. This finding indicates that classrooms having higher scores on global classroom quality had lower scores on the Red Flags subscale. Overall ECERS-R scores had noteworthy relationships with 10 of the 14 key practice items on the TPOT. Correlations

Table 7.13. Correlation coefficients between ECERS-R subscales and overall ECERS-R score with Teaching Pyramid Observation Tool (TPOT™) variables: Research edition of TPOT (n = 40)

ECERS-R subscale	SR	TR	SC	ENG	PD	CT	TBE	TSC	TEE	TPS	FR	PCB	COM	INF	KP	RF
													TPOT variables			
Space and furnishings	.41**	.30	.32*	.39*	.14	.04	.37*	.30	.25	.48**	.30	.39*	.33*	.45**	.48**	−.46**
Personal care routines	.33*	.23	.38*	.48**	.21	.17	.34*	.49**	.42**	.61**	.54**	.24	.14	.49**	.55**	−.51**
Language and reasoning	.44**	.28	.38*	.47**	.13	.20	.24	.34*	.46**	.24	.25	.22	.16	.36*	.45**	−.38**
Activities	.38*	.25	.28	.44**	.15	.23	.51**	.30	.39*	.39*	.31*	.21	.14	.52**	.49**	−.47**
Interaction	.27	.19	.29	.48**	.12	.15	.36*	.31	.33*	.38*	.38*	.24	−.09	.45**	.43**	−.50**
Program structure	.04	.02	.14	.33*	.15	.13	.17	.03	.24	.09	−.02	.39*	−.15	.16	.19	−.22
Parents and staff	−.02	−.05	−.01	.01	.01	−.11	−.07	−.03	−.03	.06	.02	.31	−.19	.11	.01	.01
Overall ECERS-R Score	.39*	.27	.37*	.53**	.20	.16	.42**	.36*	.42**	.49**	.38*	.42**	.10	.54**	.55**	−.53**

Note. COM = connecting with families; CT = collaborative teaming; ECERS-R = Early Childhood Environment Rating Scale– Revised; ENG = promoting engagement; FR = teaching friendship skills; INF = supporting family use of *Pyramid Model* practices; KP = key *Pyramid Model* practices subscale; PCB = interventions for children with persistent challenging behavior; PD = providing directions; RF = red flags; SC = supportive conversations; SR = schedules, routines, and activities; TBE = teaching behavior expectations; TEE = teaching children to express emotions; TPS = teaching problem solving; TR = transitions between activities; TSC = teaching social skills and emotional competencies.
$*p < .05, **p < .01.$

between five of the seven ECERS-R subscales (i.e., variables other than program structure and parents and staff) and the Key Practices subscale were moderate, ranging from 0.43 to 0.55. There were noteworthy relationships between all but one of the ECERS-R subscales and the engagement key practice item on the TPOT. For the supporting family use of key practices items, there were noteworthy correlations with five of the seven ECERS-R subscales.

To conduct exploratory analyses with the CLASS, we used data from the pilot version of the TPOT (n = 90 classrooms). Correlation coefficients are shown in Table 7.14. The Key Practices subscale has substantial positive relationships with all CLASS domain and dimension scores. Red flags have substantial negative relationships with all CLASS domain and dimension scores, indicating that higher CLASS scores were associated with lower red flag scores. The items on collaborative teaming and interventions for children with persistent challenging behavior generally had the weakest relationships with CLASS variables. Key practice items related to general teaching practices (i.e., schedules, routines, and activities; transitions, supportive conversations, engagement, providing directions) and the key practice item related to connecting with families tended to be substantially correlated with all CLASS domains and dimensions. All but one TPOT key practice item had noteworthy relationships with the classroom organization domain on the CLASS. The supportive conversations item is the TPOT item that had the strongest relationship with the CLASS emotional support domain and its dimensions. TPOT items focused on teaching social and emotional skills and supporting family use of *Pyramid Model* practices tended to have their highest correlations with the CLASS instructional support domain and its dimensions.

To What Extent Are TPOT Scores Related to Scores on Other Instruments Designed to Measure Program-Wide Positive Behavior Support?

Steed and Pomerleau (2012) reported on a study conducted to evaluate relationships between scores on the Preschool-Wide Evaluation Tool (PreSET™) and the 2008 pilot version of the TPOT (Fox, Hemmeter, & Snyder, 2008). The PreSET is a measure designed to evaluate the universal level of program-wide implementation of positive

Table 7.14.   Correlation coefficients for CLASS and TPOT variables: Pilot version of TPOT (n = 90)

CLASS variables	TPOT variables															
	SR	TR	SC	ENG	PD	CT	TBE	TSC	TEE	TPS	FR	PCB	COM	INF	KP	RF
ES	.51**	.42**	.70**	.59**	.50**	.22*	.21*	.31**	.30**	.29**	.20	.29**	.43**	.30**	.63**	−.62**
PC	.46**	.39**	.65**	.55**	.45**	.23*	.16	.27*	.25*	.22*	.19	.35**	.44**	.28**	.58**	−.53**
NC	.41**	.27**	.63**	.53**	.46**	.09	.12	.21*	.20	.16	.06	.18	.27**	.16	.45**	−.57**
TS	.51**	.41**	.63**	.54**	.49**	.21*	.22*	.26*	.26*	.30**	.22*	.31**	.40**	.31**	.60**	−.54**
RFS	.46**	.44**	.61**	.49**	.41**	.27**	.25*	.37**	.39**	.38**	.25*	.19	.42**	.34**	.63**	−.59**
CO	.45**	.46**	.59**	.57**	.49**	.19	.27**	.33**	.25*	.31**	.29**	.25*	.41**	.30**	.61**	−.53**
BM	.41**	.40**	.57**	.49**	.37**	.16	.19	.31**	.23*	.26*	.26*	.25*	.35**	.31**	.54**	−.50**
PR	.40**	.43**	.47**	.54**	.42**	.09	.23*	.27**	.18	.23*	.26*	.16	.34**	.20	.51**	−.49**
ILF	.41**	.41**	.54**	.52**	.53**	.24*	.30**	.31**	.27*	.34**	.27*	.26*	.41**	.29**	.60**	−.45**
IS	.44**	.55**	.55**	.42**	.40**	.23*	.33**	.47**	.49**	.52**	.41**	.26*	.43**	.42**	.70**	−.48**
CD	.46**	.55**	.46**	.44**	.47**	.12	.42**	.41**	.44**	.42**	.32**	.18	.40**	.28**	.64**	−.39**
QOF	.40**	.47**	.49**	.36**	.34**	.26*	.30**	.42**	.43**	.47**	.41**	.27**	.42**	.38**	.64**	−.41**
LM	.39**	.50**	.54**	.38**	.34**	.22*	.24*	.46**	.47**	.53**	.38**	.25*	.36**	.47**	.66**	−.51**

Note. BM = behavior management; CD = concept development; CLASS = Classroom Assessment Scoring System; CO = classroom organization; COM = connecting with families; CT = collaborative teaming; ENG = promoting engagement; ES = emotional support; FR = teaching friendship skills; ILF = instructional learning formats; INF = supporting family use of *Pyramid Model* practices; IS = instructional support; KP = key *Pyramid Model* practices subscale; LM, language modeling; NC = negative climate; PC = positive climate; PCB = interventions for children with persistent challenging behavior; PD = providing directions; PR = productivity; QF = quality of feedback; RF = red flags; RFS = regard for student perspectives; SC = supportive conversations; SR = schedules, routines, and activities; TBE = teaching behavior expectations; TEE = teaching children to express emotions; TPS = teaching problem solving; TR = transitions between activities; TS = teacher sensitivity; TSC = teaching social skills and emotional competencies.
*p < .05. **p < .01.

behavior intervention and support in early childhood programs and builds upon a framework provided by the School-Wide Evaluation Tool (SET; Sugai, Lewis-Palmer, Todd, & Horner, 2001). Although the PreSET generally follows the structure and scoring of the SET, items were added or modified for application in early childhood settings (Steed & Pomerleau, 2012).

The PreSET includes eight subscales: 1) expectations defined, 2) behavioral expectations taught, 3) responses to appropriate and challenging behavior, 4) organized and predictable environment, 5) monitoring and decision making, 6) family involvement, 7) management, and 8) program support. Interviews and observations are organized around these eight subscales and are conducted in each classroom in an early childhood program. Classroom scores are summarized on a classroom summary form and scores from an administrator interview form are transferred to a scoring guide and are used to calculate a percent-implemented score for each of the eight subscales (Steed & Pomerleau, 2012).

To evaluate relationships between PreSET and TPOT scores, Steed and Pomerleau (2012) reported that both instruments were administered in 31 early childhood classrooms in the southeastern United States. Sixteen of these classrooms were state-funded preschool classrooms and 15 were private childcare classrooms. Examiners were trained to administer both instruments and had to obtain at least 85% reliability. Total scores on the two instruments were modestly and positively correlated ($r = 0.33$). Table 7.15 shows PreSET subscales and TPOT key practice items that were positively and moderately correlated. There generally were not noteworthy relationships between TPOT key practice items and the monitoring and decision making or program support subscales on the PreSET (correlations ranged between −0.33 to 0.29). Steed and Pomerleau noted that these results demonstrate both initial convergent score validity between the TPOT and PreSET as fidelity of implementation measures related to positive behavior support and intervention and divergent score validity for constructs that are not common to both tools (e.g., monitoring, decision making).

Table 7.15. PreSET and select TPOT key practice items correlations: Pilot version of TPOT in 31 classrooms

PreSET subscale	TPOT item	Correlations
Expectations defined	Teaching children behavior expectations	.41*
Expectations taught	Teaching children behavior expectations	.25
Responses to appropriate and challenging behavior	Supportive conversations	.52**
	Responding to problem behavior	.58**
	Classroom environments[a]	.45*
	Schedules and routines	.52**
Organized and predictable environments	Transitions	.55**
Family involvement	Supporting family use of *Pyramid Model* practices	.19

Note. Adapted with permission from Steed and Pomerleau (2012). PreSET = Preschool-Wide Evaluation Tool; TPOT™ = Teaching Pyramid Observation Tool.

[a]Seven environmental items were included in the pilot version of the TPOT.

*p < .05. **p < .01.

To What Extent Are TPOT Scores Sensitive to Detecting Change in Preschool Teachers' Implementation of Pyramid Model Practices?

We used data from the pilot version of the TPOT collected in Study 2 (i.e., the potential efficacy study) to examine change in implementation of *Pyramid Model* practices across treatment and control groups. Figure 7.1 shows mean scores for these two groups at each of the four measurement occasions of the study on the Key Practices subscale. All items except promoting children's engagement, connecting with families, and supporting family use of *Pyramid Model* practices had significant differences between groups by the fourth measurement occasion. Means for the control group were fairly stable over the four waves; means for the treatment group increased steadily over the course of the study. Error bars were constructed so that nonoverlapping bars indicate significant differences between the groups at measurement occasions 3 and 4. All items except promoting children's

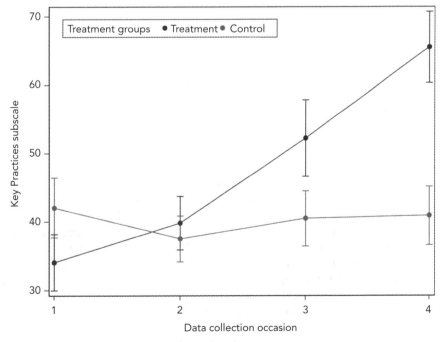

Figure 7.1. Mean results by group and data collection occasion: Key Practices subscale.

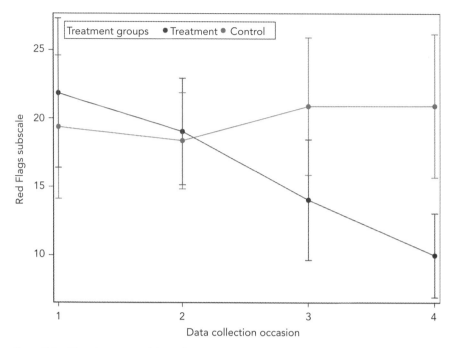

Figure 7.2.   Means by group and data collection occasion: Red Flags subscale.

engagement, connecting with families, and supporting family use of *Pyramid Model* practices had significant differences between groups by the fourth measurement occasion.

Figure 7.2 shows mean scores for these two groups at each of the four measurement occasions on the Red Flags subscale. Red flags subscale means for the control group were fairly stable over time; means for the treatment group decreased steadily over the course of the study, which is a positive finding given that red flag practices are inconsistent with fidelity of implementation of *Pyramid Model* practices. Error bars for red flags indicate significant differences between the groups at the fourth measurement occasion.

What Is the Relationship Between Teachers' Implementation of Pyramid Model Practices and Children's Social Skills and Challenging Behavior?

Data collected in Study 2 (i.e., the potential efficacy study) included scores on the social skills and problem behavior subscales of the SSIS (Gresham & Elliott, 2008). We investigated the relationship of implementation of *Pyramid Model* practices and these two subscales. A multilevel analysis using data for all children in the study on the postintervention occasion ($n = 434$) showed that scores on the Key Practices subscale were significantly and positively related to scores on the social skills subscale ($t[38] = 2.28$, $p = .03$). Data for both variables were collected on the fourth measurement occasion. Because the Key Practices subscale describes teachers' implementation of *Pyramid Model* practices, a positive relationship would imply that classrooms of teachers who implemented *Pyramid Model* practices more effectively tended to include children with higher average social skills scores. The pseudo R^2 statistic was 0.12 and indicates that Key Practices subscale scores accounted for 12% of the variance in class-average social skills scores. The Red Flags subscale was significantly negatively related to scores on the social skills subscale ($t[38] = -2.16$, $p = .04$). Pseudo R^2 indicated that red flags scores accounted for

7% of the variance in class-average social skills scores. Neither Key Practices subscale nor Red Flags subscale scores were significant predictors of children's problem behavior scores. As part of Study 3, we will explore further relationships between teachers' implementation of *Pyramid Model* practices and children's social skills and challenging behavior with larger samples of teachers and children, as well as examine the relationships between teachers' implementation of *Pyramid Model* practices and children's preacademic and communication skills.

References

Achenbach, T., & Rescorla, L. (2000). *Achenbach system of empirically based assessment: Caregiver-teacher report form for ages 1½–5*. Burlington, VT: Achenbach System of Empirically Based Assessment.

American Educational Research Association, American Psychological Association, & National Council on Measurement in Education. (1999). *Standards for educational and psychological testing*. Washington, DC: American Educational Research Association.

Artman-Meeker, K., & Hemmeter, M.L. (2013). Effects of training and feedback on teachers' use of classroom preventive practices. *Topics in Early Childhood Special Education, 13*, 112–123.

Artman-Meeker, K.M., Hemmeter, M.L., & Snyder, P. (2013). Effects of distance coaching on teachers' use of a tiered model of intervention. Manuscript submitted for publication.

Birch, S.H., & Ladd, G.W. (1998). Children's interpersonal behaviors and the teacher-child relationship. *Developmental Psychology, 34*(5), 934–946.

Blair, K.S.C., Fox, L., & Lentini, R. (2010). Use of positive behavior support to address the challenging behavior of young children within a community early childhood program. *Topics in Early Childhood Special Education, 30*, 68–79.

Bodrova, E., & Leong, D.J. (1998). Learning and development of preschool children from the Vygotskian perspective. In A. Kozulin, B. Gindis, V.S. Ageyev, & S.M. Miller (Eds.), *Vygotsky's educational theory in cultural context* (pp.156–176). Cambridge, UK: Cambridge University Press.

Bodrova, E., & Leong, D.J. (2007). *Tools of the mind: The Vygotskian approach to early childhood education* (2nd ed.). New York, NY: Merrill/Prentice-Hall.

Branson, D., & Demchak, M.A. (2011). Toddler teachers' use of teaching pyramid practices. *Topics in Early Childhood Special Education, 30*(4), 196–208.

Brown, W.H., Odom, S.L., & McConnell, S.R. (2008). *Social competence of young children, risk, disability, and intervention*. Baltimore, MD: Paul H. Brookes Publishing Co.

Burchinal, M., Vandergrift, N., Pianta, R., & Mashburn, A. (2010). Threshold analysis of association between child care quality and child outcomes for low income children in pre-kindergarten programs. *Early Childhood Research Quarterly, 25*, 166–176.

Center on Social and Emotional Foundations for Early Learning at Vanderbilt University. (2003). *Pyramid model for promoting social and emotional competence in infants and young children*. Nashville, TN: Author.

Chandler, L.K., Dahlquist, C.M., Repp, A.C., & Feltz, C. (1999). The effects of team-based functional assessment on the behavior of students in classroom settings. *Exceptional Children, 66*, 101–122.

Chien, N.C., Howes, C., Burchinal, M., Pianta, R.C., Ritchie, S., Bryant, D.M., & Barbarin, O.A. (2010). Children's classroom engagement and school readiness gains in pre-kindergarten. *Child Development, 81*, 1534–1549.

Coie, J.D., & Koeppl, G.K. (1990). Adapting intervention to the problems of aggressive and disruptive rejected children. In S.R. Asher & J.D. Coie (Eds.), *Peer rejection in childhood* (pp. 309–337). New York, NY: Cambridge University Press.

Conroy, M.A., Brown, W.H., & Olive, M.L. (2008). Social competence interventions for young children with challenging behavior. In W.H. Brown, S.L. Odom, & S.R. McConnell (Eds.), *Social competence of young children. risk, disability, and intervention* (pp. 205–232). Baltimore, MD: Paul H. Brookes Publishing Co.

Conroy, M.A., Dunlap, G., Clarke, S., & Alter, P.J. (2005). A descriptive analysis of behavioral intervention research with young children with challenging behavior. *Topics in Early Childhood Special Education, 25*, 157–166.

Cox, D.D. (2005). Evidence-based interventions using home-school collaboration. *School Psychology Quarterly, 20,* 473–497.

Crocker, L., & Algina, J. (2008). *Introduction to classical and modern test theory.* Belmont, CA: Wadsworth.

Cronbach, L.J., Gleser, G.C., Nanda, H., & Rajaratnam, N. (1972). *The dependability of behavioral measurements: Theory of generalizability of scores and profiles.* New York, NY: Wiley.

DeKlyen, M., & Odom, S.L. (1989). Activity structure and social interactions with peers in developmentally integrated play groups. *Journal of Early Intervention, 13,* 342–352.

Denham, S.A., & Burton, R. (1996). A social-emotional intervention for at-risk 4-year-olds. *Journal of School Psychology, 34,* 225–245.

Duda, M.A., Dunlap, G., Fox, L., Lentini, R., & Clarke, S. (2004). An experimental evaluation of positive behavior support in a community preschool program. *Topics in Early Childhood Special Education, 24,* 143–155.

Dunlap, G., Strain, P.S., Fox, L., Carta, J., Conroy, M., Smith, B. J....& Sowell, C. (2006). Prevention and intervention with young children's challenging behavior: A summary of current knowledge. *Behavioral Disorders, 32,* 29–45.

Dunlap, G., Wilson, K., Strain, P., & Lee, J.K. (2013). *Prevent-Teach-Reinforce for young children: The early childhood model of individualized positive behavior support.* Baltimore, MD: Paul H. Brookes Publishing Co.

Fox, L., Carta, J., Strain, P.S., Dunlap, G., & Hemmeter, M.L. (2010). Response to intervention and the pyramid model. *Infants and Young Children, 23,* 3–14.

Fox, L., & Clarke, S. (2006). Aggression? Using positive behavior support to address challenging behavior. *Young Exceptional Children Monograph Series, 8,* 42–56.

Fox, L., Dunlap, G., & Cushing, L. (2002). Early intervention, positive behavior support, and transition to school. *Journal of Emotional and Behavior Disorders, 10*(3), 149–157.

Fox, L., Dunlap, G., Hemmeter, M.L., Joseph, G.E., & Strain, P.S. (2003). The teaching pyramid: A model for supporting social competence and preventing challenging behavior in young children. *Young Children, 58,* 48–52.

Fox, L., Hemmeter, M.L., & Snyder, P. (2008). *Teaching pyramid observation tool for preschool classrooms: Pilot version.* Unpublished instrument and manual.

Fox, L., Hemmeter, M.L., & Snyder, P. (2009). *Teaching pyramid observation tool for preschool classrooms: Pilot version.* Unpublished instrument and manual.

Fox, L., Hemmeter, M.L., Snyder, P.S., Binder, D.P., & Clarke, S. (2011). Coaching early childhood special educators to implement a comprehensive model for the promotion of young children's social competence. *Topics in Early Childhood Special Education, 31,* 178–192.

Frede, E.C., Austin, A.B., & Lindauer, S.K. (1993). The relationship of specific developmentally appropriate teaching practices to children's skills in first grade. *Advances in Early Education and Child Care, 5,* 95–111.

Gordon, R.S. (1983). An operational classification of disease prevention. *Public Health Reports, 98,* 107–109.

Greenwood, C. (2009). Treatment integrity: Revisiting some big ideas. *School Psychology Review, 38,* 547–569.

Gresham, F.M., & Elliott, S.N. (2008). *Social skills improvement system: Rating scales.* Bloomington, MN: Pearson Assessments.

Grisham-Brown, J.L., Hemmeter, M.L., & Pretti-Frontczak, K.L. (2005). *Blended practices in early childhood and early childhood special education.* Baltimore, MD: Paul H. Brookes Publishing Co.

Harms, T., Clifford, R.M., & Cryer, D. (2005). *Early childhood environment rating scale* (Revised ed.). New York, NY: Teachers College Press.

Hemmeter, M.L., Fox, L., Snyder, P., & Algina, J. (2012). *Examining the efficacy of a classroom-wide model for promoting social emotional development and addressing challenging behavior in preschool children with or at-risk for disabilities.* Retrieved from http://ies.ed.gov/funding/grantsearch/details.asp?ID=1246.

Hemmeter, M.L., Ostrosky, M., & Fox, L. (2006). Social and emotional foundations for early learning: A conceptual model for intervention. *School Psychology Review, 35,* 583–601.

Hemmeter, M.L., Snyder, P., Fox, L., & Algina, J. (2011, April). *Efficacy of a classroom wide model for promoting social-emotional development and preventing challenging behavior.* Paper presented at the annual meeting of the American Educational Research Association. New Orleans, LA.

Holloway, S.D., & Reichart-Erickson, M. (1988). The relationship of day care quality to children's free play behavior and social problem-solving skills. *Early Childhood Research Quarterly, 3,* 39–53.

Horner, R.H., Sugai, G., Todd, A.W., & Lewis-Palmer, T. (2005). School-wide positive behavior support. In L.M. Bambara & L. Kern (Eds.), *Individualized supports for students with problem behaviors: Designing positive behavior plans* (pp. 359–390). New York, NY: Guilford Press.

Howes, C., & Hamilton, C.E. (1993). The changing experience of child care: Changes in teachers and in teacher-child relationships and children's social competence with peers. *Early Childhood Research Quarterly, 8*, 15–32.

Howes, C., & Smith, E.W. (1995). Relations among child care quality, teacher behavior, children's play activities, emotional security, and cognitive activity in child care. *Early Childhood Research Quarterly, 10*, 381–404.

Jolivette, K., Wehby, J.H., Canale, J., & Massey, N.G. (2001). Effects of choice making opportunities on the behaviors of students with emotional and behavioral disorders. *Behavioral Disorders, 26*, 131–145.

Joseph, G.E., & Strain, P.S. (2003). Comprehensive evidence-based social-emotional curricula for young children: An analysis of efficacious adoption potential. *Topics in Early Childhood Special Education, 23*, 65–76.

Kontos, S. (1999). Preschool teachers' talk, roles, and activity settings during free play. *Early Childhood Research Quarterly, 14*, 363–382.

McLaren, E.M., & Nelson, C.M. (2009). Using functional behavior assessment to develop behavior interventions for children in Head Start. *Journal of Positive Behavior Interventions, 11*, 3–21.

Messick, S. (1993). Validity. In R.L. Linn (Ed.), *Educational measurement* (3rd ed., pp. 13–104). Washington, DC: American Council on Education.

Mill, D., & Romano-White, D. (1999). Correlates of affectionate and angry behavior in child care educators of preschool-aged children. *Early Childhood Research Quarterly, 14*, 155–178.

Mize, J., & Ladd, G.W. (1990). Toward the development of successful social skills training for preschool children. In S.R. Asher & J.D. Coie (Eds.), *Peer rejection in childhood* (pp. 338–361). New York, NY: Cambridge University Press.

Morris, J. (2012). *Assessing the effectiveness of individualized behavior support interventions for children with challenging behavior in early care and education environments.* Unpublished doctoral dissertation, Vanderbilt University.

National Center on Quality Teaching and Learning (2013). *Practice-based coaching.* Retrieved from http://eclkc.ohs.acf.hhs.gov/hslc/tta-system/teaching/docs/practice-based-coaching.pdf

National Research Council. (2001). *Eager to learn: Educating our preschoolers.* Washington, DC: National Academies Press.

National Research Council. (2008). *Early childhood assessment: Why, what, and how.* Washington, DC: National Academies Press.

National Training Institute. (2013, March). *Teaching pyramid observation tool reliability training.* Preconference training workshop presented at the 10th annual National Training Institute on Effective Practices, Clearwater Beach, FL.

Peisner-Feinberg, E.S., Burchinal, M.R., Clifford, R.M., Yazejian, N., Culkin, M.L., Zelazo, J., Rustici, J. (2000). *The children of the cost, quality, and outcomes go to school: Technical report.* Chapel Hill, NC: University of North Carolina at Chapel Hill, Frank Porter Graham Child Development Center.

Pianta, R.C., La Paro, K.M., & Hamre, B.K. (2008). *Classroom assessment scoring system manual: Pre-K.* Baltimore, MD: Paul H. Brookes Publishing Co.

Pianta, R.C., Steinberg, M., & Rollins, K. (1995). The first two years of school: Teacher child relationships and deflections in children's classroom adjustment. *Developmental and Psychopathology, 7*, 295–312.

Powell, D.R., & Diamond, K.E. (2013). Studying the implementation of coaching-based professional development. In T. Halle, A. Metz, & I. Martinez-Beck (Eds.), *Applying implementation science in early childhood programs and systems* (pp. 97-116). Baltimore, MD: Paul H. Brookes Publishing Co..

Powell, D., Dunlap, G., & Fox, L. (2006). Prevention and intervention for the challenging behaviors of toddlers and preschoolers. *Infants and Young Children, 19*(1), 25–35.

Quesenberry, A.C., Hemmeter, M.L., & Ostrosky, M.M. (2011). Addressing challenging behavior in Head Start: A closer look at program policies and procedures. *Topics in Early Childhood Special Education, 30*, 209–220.

Reichle, J., McEvoy, M., Davis, C., Rogers, E., Feeley, K., Johnston, S., & Wolff, K. (1996). Coordinating preservice and in-service training of early interventionists to serve preschoolers who engage in challenging behavior. In L. K. Koegel, R.L. Koegel, & G. Dunlap (Eds.), *Positive behavioral support: Including people with difficult behavior in the community* (pp. 227–264). Baltimore, MD: Paul H Brookes Publishing Co.

Schneider, J. (1974). Turtle technique in the classroom. *Teaching Exceptional Children, 7*, 21–24.

Schnitz, A., Hemmeter, M. L., Hardy, J. K., Adams, J. M., & Kinder, K. (2011, November). *Supporting teacher implementation of Teaching Pyramid Strategies: Research on coaching with performance feedback.* Paper presented at the Annual DEC International Conference on Young Children with Special Needs and their Families, National Harbor, MD.

Serna, L., Nielsen, E., Lambros, K., & Forness, S. (2000). Primary prevention with children at risk for emotional or behavioral disorders: Data on a universal intervention for head start classrooms. *Behavioral Disorders, 26*(1), 70–84.

Shavelson, R.J., & Webb, N.M. (1991). *Generalizability theory: A primer.* Thousand Oaks, CA: Sage.

Shure, M.B., & Spivack, G. (1980). Interpersonal problem solving as a mediator of behavioral adjustment in preschool and kindergarten children. *Journal of Applied Developmental Psychology, 1*, 29–44.

Simeonsson, R.J. (1991). Primary, secondary, and tertiary prevention in early intervention. *Journal of Early Intervention, 15*, 124–134.

Snell, M.E., Berlin, R.A., Voorhees, M.D., Stanton-Chapman, T.L., & Hadden, S. (2012). A survey of preschool classroom staff concerning problem behavior and its prevention in head start classrooms. *Journal of Positive Behavior Interventions, 14*(2), 98–107.

Snell, M.E., Voorhees, M.D., Berlin, R.A., Stanton-Chapman, T.L., Hadden, S., & McCarty, S. (2012). Use of interview and observation to clarify reported practices of head start staff concerning problem behavior: Implications for programs and training. *Journal of Positive Behavior Interventions, 14*(2), 108–117.

Snow, C.E., & VanHemel, S.B. (2008). (Eds.). *Early childhood assessment: What, why, and how.* Washington, DC: National Academies Press.

Snyder, P., Hemmeter, M.L., McLaughlin, T., Algina, J., Sandall, S., & McLean, M. (2011, April). *Impact of professional development on preschool teachers' use of embedded instruction practices.* Paper presented at the annual meeting of the American Educational Research Association, New Orleans, LA.

Snyder, P., McLean, M., & Bailey, D.B. (2013). Types and technical characteristics of assessment instruments. In M. McLean, M.L. Hemmeter, & P. Snyder (Eds.), *Essential elements for assessing infants and preschoolers with special needs.* Boston, MA: Pearson.

Steed, E.A., & Durand, V.M. (2013). Optimistic teaching: Improving the capacity for teachers to reduce young children's challenging behavior. *School Mental Health, 5*(1), 15–24.

Steed, E.A., & Pomerleau, T.M. (2012). *Preschool-wide evaluation tool (PreSET) manual: Assessing universal program-wide positive behavior support in early childhood* (Research ed.). Baltimore, MD: Paul H. Brookes Publishing Co.

Sugai, G., Lewis-Palmer, T.J., Todd, A., & Horner, R.H. (2001). *School-wide evaluation tool.* Eugene, OR: University of Oregon

Thompson, B. (2003). *Score reliability: Contemporary thinking on reliability issues.* Thousand Oaks, CA: Sage.

Vaughn, S., Kim, A., Sloan, C.V.M., Hughes, M.T., Elbaum, B., & Sridhar, D. (2003). Social skills interventions for young children with disabilities: A synthesis of group design studies. *Remedial and Special Education, 24*, 2–15.

Vaughn, S.R., & Ridley, C.R. (1983). A preschool interpersonal problem solving program: Does it affect behavior in the classroom? *Child Study Journal, 13*(1), 1–11.

Walker, H.M., Horner, R.H., Sugai, G., Bullis, M., Sprague, J.R., Bricker, D., & Kaufman, M.J. (1996). Integrated approaches to preventing antisocial behavior patterns among school-age children and youth. *Journal of Emotional and Behavioral Disorders, 4*, 194–209.

Webster-Stratton, C., Reid, M.J., & Hammond, M. (2001). Preventing conduct problems, promoting social competence: A parent and teacher training partnership in head start. *Journal of Clinical Child and Adolescent Psychology, 30*, 283–302.

Wolery, M. (2011). Intervention research: The importance of fidelity measurement. *Topics in Early Childhood Special Education, 31*, 155–157.

Related Readings and Resources

PYRAMID MODEL

Blair, K., Fox, L., & Lentini, R. (2010). Positive behavior support for young children with developmental and behavioral challenges: An evaluation of generalization. *Topics in Early Childhood Special Education, 30*(2), 68–79.

Dunlap, G., & Fox, L. (2009). Positive behavior support and early intervention. In W. Sailor, G. Dunlap, G. Sugai, & R. Horner (Eds.), *Handbook of positive behavior support* (pp. 49–72). New York, NY: Springer.

Dunlap, G., & Fox, L. (2011). Function-based interventions for children with challenging behavior. *Journal of Early Intervention, 33,* 333–343.

Dunlap, G., Strain, P.S., Fox, L., Carta, J., Conroy, M., Smith, B., et al. (2006). Prevention and intervention with young children's challenging behavior: A summary of current knowledge. *Behavioral Disorders, 32,* 29–45.

Dunlap, G., Wilson, K., Strain, P., & Lee, J.K. (2013). *Prevent-Teach-Reinforce for young children: The early childhood model of individualized positive behavior support.* Baltimore, MD: Paul H. Brookes Publishing Co.

Fox, L., Carta, J., Dunlap, G., Strain, P., & Hemmeter, M.L. (2010). Response to intervention and the Pyramid Model. *Infants and Young Children, 23,* 3–14.

Fox, L., & Clarke, S. (2006). Aggression? Using positive behavior support to address challenging behavior. *Young Exceptional Children Monograph Series, 8,* 42–56.

Fox, L., Dunlap, G., Hemmeter, M.L., Joseph, G.E., & Strain, P.S. (2003). The teaching pyramid: A model for supporting social competence and preventing challenging behavior in young children. *Young Children, 58,* 48–52.

Fox, L., & Hemmeter, M.L. (2009).A program-wide model for supporting social emotional development and addressing challenging behavior in early childhood settings. In W. Sailor, G. Dunlap, G. Sugai, & R. Horner (Eds.), *Handbook of positive behavior support* (pp. 177–202). New York, NY: Springer.

Fox, L., & Lentini, R.H. (2006). You got it!: Teaching social and emotional skills. *Young Children, 61*(6), 36–42.

Hemmeter, M.L., & Conroy, M. (2012). Supporting the social competence of young children with challenging behavior in the context of the Teaching Pyramid model: Research-based practices and implementation in early childhood settings. In R. Pianta, L. Justice, S. Barnett, & S. Sheridan (Eds.), *The handbook of early education* (pp. 416–434). New York, NY: Guilford.

Hemmeter, M.L., & Fox, L., (2009). The Teaching Pyramid: A model for the implementation of classroom practices within a program-wide approach to behavior support. *NHSA Dialogue, 12,* 133–147.

Hemmeter, M.L., Fox, L., & Doubet, S. (2006). Together we can: An early childhood center's program-wide approach to addressing challenging behavior. *Young Exceptional Children Monograph Series, 8,* 1–14.

Hemmeter, M.L., Fox, L., Jack, S., Broyles, L., & Doubet, S. (2007). A program-wide model of positive behavior support in early childhood settings. *Journal of Early Intervention, 29,* 337–355.

Hemmeter, M.L., Fox, L., & Snyder, P. (2013). A tiered model for promoting social-emotional competence and addressing challenging behavior. In V. Buysse & E.S. Peisner-Feinberg (Eds.), *Handbook of response to intervention in early childhood* (pp. 85–101). Baltimore, MD: Paul H. Brookes Publishing Co.

Hemmeter, M.L., Ostrosky, L., Artman, K., & Kinder, K. (2008). Moving right along: Planning transitions to prevent challenging behavior. *Young Children, 63*(3), 18–25.

Hemmeter, M.L., Ostrosky, M., & Corso, R. (2012). Preventing and addressing challenging behavior: Common questions and practical solutions. *Young Exceptional Children, 15,* 31–44.

Hemmeter, M.L., Ostrosky, M., & Fox, L. (2006). Social and emotional foundations for early learning: A conceptual model for intervention. *School Psychology Review, 35*(4), 583–601.

Hunter, A., & Hemmeter, M.L. (2009). The Center on the Social and Emotional Foundations for Early Learning: Addressing challenging behaviors in infants and toddlers. *Zero to Three, 29*(3), 5–12.

Joseph, G.E., & Strain, P.S. (2002a). Building positive relationships with young children. *Young Exceptional Children, 7*(4), 21–28.

Joseph, G.E., & Strain, P.S. (2002b). Helping young children control anger and handle disappointment. *Young Exceptional Children, 7*(1), 21–29.

Joseph, G.E., & Strain, P.S. (2003). Enhancing emotional vocabulary in young children. *Young Exceptional Children, 6*(4), 18–26.

Strain, P.S., Joseph, G., & Hemmeter, M.L. (2009). Young children's problem behavior: Impact intervention and innovations. *Early Childhood Services, 3*, 1–14.

Strain, P., Wilson, K., & Dunlap, G. (2011). Prevent-Teach-Reinforce: Addressing problem behaviors of students with autism in general education classrooms. *Behavioral Disorders, 36*, 160–171.

PROFESSIONAL DEVELOPMENT

Artman, K., & Hemmeter, M.L. (2013). Effects of training and feedback on teachers' use of classroom preventive practices. *Topics in Early Childhood Special Education, 13*, 112–123.

Barton, E.E., Kinder, K., Casey, A.M., & Artman, K.M. (2011). Finding your feedback fit: Strategies for designing and delivering performance feedback systems. *Young Exceptional Children, 14*, 29–46.

Fox, L., & Hemmeter, M.L. (2011). Coaching early educators to implement effective practices. *Zero to Three, 32*(2), 18–24.

Fox, L., Hemmeter, M.L., Snyder, P., Binder, D., & Clarke, S. (2011). Coaching early childhood educators to implement a comprehensive model for the promotion of young children's social competence. *Topics in Early Childhood Special Education, 31*, 178–192.

Hemmeter, M.L., & Fox, L. (2007). Supporting teachers in promoting children's social competence and addressing challenging behavior. In P.J. Winton, J.A. McCollum, & C. Catlett (Eds.), *Practical approaches to early childhood professional development: Evidence, strategies, and resources* (pp. 119–141). Washington, DC: ZERO TO THREE.

Hemmeter, M.L., Santos, R., & Ostrosky, M. (2008). A national survey of higher education programs: Preparing early childhood educators to address social emotional development and challenging behavior. *Journal of Early Intervention, 30*(4), 321–340.

Hemmeter, M.L., Snyder, P., Kinder, K., & Artman, K. (2011). Impact of performance feedback delivered via electronic mail on preschool teachers' use of descriptive praise. *Early Childhood Research Quarterly, 26*, 96–109.

Snyder, P., Denney, M., Pasia, C., Rakap, S., & Crowe, C. (2011). Professional development in early childhood intervention: Emerging issues and promising approaches. In C. Groark (Series Ed.) & L. Kaczmarek (Vol. Ed.), *Early childhood intervention: Shaping the future for children with special needs and their families: Vol. 3. Emerging trends in research and practice* (pp.169–204). Santa Barbara, CA: Praeger/ABC-CLIO.

Snyder, P., Hemmeter, M.L., Artman, K., Kinder, K., Pasia, C., & McLaughlin, T. (2012). Characterizing key features of the early childhood professional development literature. *Infants and Young Children, 25*, 188–212.

Snyder, P., Hemmeter, M.L., & McLaughlin, T. (2011). Professional development in early childhood intervention: Where we stand on the silver anniversary of P.L. 99–457. *Journal of Early Intervention, 33*, 357–370.

WEB SITES

Center on the Social Emotional Foundations for Early Learning (http://csefel.vanderbilt.edu): Resources include training modules, parent training modules, parent articles, practical strategies for classroom implementation, *Pyramid Model* briefs, training kits, *Pyramid Model* videos, and more.

Technical Assistance Center on Social Emotional Intervention for Young Children (http://www.challengingbehavior.org): Resources include *Pyramid Model* fact sheets, training materials, coaching resources, demonstration site video clips, webinars, materials for families, and information for administrators.

Frequently Asked Questions

1. HOW IS THE TPOT DIFFERENT FROM OTHER CLASSROOM OBSERVATION TOOLS?

The TPOT is designed to measure the implementation of classroom practices specifically related to promoting young children's social-emotional competence and addressing challenging behavior in preschool classrooms. It was purposefully designed as a tool that would complement but be distinct from existing tools focused on global classroom quality, literacy practices, or general teaching and instructional quality. Thus, it is a targeted tool that provides information on the use of specific evidence-informed practices related to social-emotional competence and challenging behavior and emphasizes practices associated with the *Pyramid Model*.

2. WHO CAN ADMINISTER A TPOT?

The TPOT should be administered by a trained administrator. We recommend that those who use the TPOT have foundational knowledge in early childhood and be able to identify factors that define quality in early childhood education settings. Users should also have knowledge about the *Pyramid Model* and associated practices. Training consists of attending a training workshop, achieving 80% agreement with the master coder by scoring a TPOT video, and achieving recommended interrater agreement criteria when using the TPOT in the field on three occasions (see Chapter 7 for these criteria).

3. HOW LONG DOES IT TAKE TO ADMINISTER THE TPOT?

Administration of the TPOT includes a 2-hour classroom observation and a 15- to 20-minute interview with the lead teacher of the classroom. Scoring, which occurs after administration, takes an additional 30–45 minutes.

4. CAN I CONDUCT THE OBSERVATION PORTION OF THE TPOT OVER SEVERAL DAYS?

The TPOT is designed to be scored based on an observation that occurs on one occasion. To score some indicators, observers must assess whether the practice associated with the indicator is used during various activities (e.g., large group, center time) occurring during a classroom day. Therefore, we recommend the TPOT observation be completed on one occasion.

5. DO I COMPLETE THE OBSERVATION OR INTERVIEW FIRST?

The interview should be conducted after the observation. This is because information from both the interview and observation can be used to score some items, and the teacher might be more comfortable sharing and clarifying information after the observation is completed.

6. CAN THE OBSERVATION AND INTERVIEW BE COMPLETED ON DIFFERENT DAYS?

The observation and interview should be conducted on the same day. There might be unusual circumstances that prevent both the observation and interview from being completed on the same day. However, the TPOT cannot be scored until both the observation and interview are completed. If both the observation and interview cannot occur on the same day, the interview should occur on the day following the observation. All items that can be scored based on the observation only should be scored on the same day as the observation.

7. CAN I SET UP A VIDEO CAMERA IN THE CLASSROOM AND THEN SCORE THE OBSERVATION PORTION USING THE VIDEO?

No. To obtain reliable and valid TPOT scores, the observation should be conducted "live" in the classroom. Scoring depends on being able to directly observe implementation of practices as teaching staff move around the classroom and interact with children. A video camera in the corner of the room will likely not capture all practices and interactions that are critical for scoring the TPOT.

8. CAN THE INTERVIEW BE CONDUCTED ON THE TELEPHONE?

We recommend that the interview be conducted in person. Again, we realize that the realities of a busy classroom might make this difficult. If the interview has to occur via phone, it should be completed not later than 1 day after the observation.

9. CAN I USE THE TPOT FOR OBSERVATIONS IN INFANT/TODDLER CLASSROOMS?

The TPOT is designed to be used in preschool classrooms. We do not recommend that it be used in classrooms serving children younger than 2 years of age. A tool is being developed that will be specifically designed for infant/toddler classrooms.

10. HOW DO I KNOW WHEN TO SCORE A RED FLAG?

Red flags are designed to be clear indicators of poor structural or process quality in the classroom environment or something that conflicts with or impedes the implementation of *Pyramid Model* practices. Thus, it should be an obvious example for it to be scored as a red flag. Specific criteria are provided in the manual and should assist in making a decision about scoring a red flag.

11. HOW DO YOU MAKE THE DECISION TO SCORE A PRACTICE AS NOT BEING OBSERVED IF THE TEACHER HAS REPORTED USE OF THE PRACTICE IN THE INTERVIEW?

The manual provides explicit instructions for how to balance teacher report with observation in terms of scoring *Yes*, *No*, or *no opportunity* (when appropriate). Generally speaking, for indicators where it is an option to score based on teacher report, you would indicate that it was reported but not observed. For indicators where teacher report is not an option, you would only be able to score indicators *Yes* if observed.

12. IF THERE ARE CO-TEACHERS IN A CLASSROOM, WHOM DO I INTERVIEW?

Your observation should be focused on the lead teacher in a preschool classroom, and the interview should be conducted with that teacher. If there are two teachers identified as having the same role in the classroom (co-teachers), you would choose one teacher to primarily focus on during the observation and interview that same teacher. If you are doing the TPOT primarily to provide feedback to both teachers, you could administer it twice, observing and interviewing each teacher on separate occasions.

13. WHAT RESOURCES ARE AVAILABLE FOR PROVIDING PROFESSIONAL DEVELOPMENT TO TEACHERS ON *PYRAMID MODEL* PRACTICES?

There are comprehensive training materials related to the *Pyramid Model* on the following web sites: http://www.challengingbehavior.org and http://www.vanderbilt.edu/csefel.

14. HOW SHOULD I APPROACH SHARING TPOT SCORES WITH TEACHERS?

This approach will depend on the purpose for which you are using the TPOT. If you are using the TPOT as a research tool, how you will share that information with teachers will depend on the consent procedures used for the research study. If you are using the TPOT as a professional development tool, we recommend sharing information from the TPOT in several ways: 1) to identify areas of strength and areas to target in professional development; 2) to share TPOT data only for items identified as a professional development focus; 3) to share TPOT data in the context of a collaborative relationship with the teacher rather than as part of job performance evaluation; 4) to relate the teachers' data to data from previous studies or to program-wide data; and (5) to show progress in practice implementation over time, particularly in relation to timing of professional development activities including coaching.

Index

Page references followed by *f* or *t* indicate figures or tables, respectively. Page references followed by *n* indicate notes.